The Reminiscences

of

Mr. Michael Bak, Jr.

U.S. Naval Institute
Annapolis, Maryland
1988

## Preface

When the men who served in destroyers in World War II get together to talk about their experiences, they have a special gleam in their eyes when they discuss the Fletcher class. These swift ships did many things and did them well. One such ship was the USS Franks (DD-554), which was in the Central Pacific campaign, the Battle of Leyte Gulf, and the final conquest of Japan. On the bridge of the Franks throughout her entire wartime service was Quartermaster Mike Bak. Just as the Franks is representative of the Fletcher class, Bak is representative of the hundreds of thousands of young men who grew up during the Depression and then went off to fight in a global war on behalf of their nation's interests.

In this memoir, Mr. Bak tells of his growing-up years in New Jersey, the widening of his horizons when he joined the Navy, the excitement of destroyer duty, and the various campaigns in which the Franks was involved.

The ship specialized in plane guard duty and rescued more than 20 downed aviators from the ocean so they could return to their carriers and to flight duty. The Franks was nearby when the escort carrier Liscome Bay was torpedoed and sunk in the Gilbert Islands campaign. The destroyer was at the Marianas in the spring of 1944 and off the Philippines in the fall of that year. At Leyte Gulf, she was among the small boys who came under fire from Japanese heavy surface combatants. Later that year, the

Franks weathered the ferocious typhoon which sank three destroyers.

In the spring of 1945, while again operating with carriers, the Franks collided with the battleship New Jersey. In the collision, the skipper of the destroyer was killed; Bak recalls his emotions at seeing his ship's commanding officer buried at sea.

In addition to the battle actions, Mr. Bak tells what destroyer life was like--the living conditions, the pleasant conversation with shipmates when off duty, going ashore in Hawaii and seeing long lines of men waiting for prostitutes, liberty in the atoll of Ulithi, and the strange experience of traveling in conquered Japan.

In the years since World War II, Mike Bak has been a successful salesman, so much so that his company recently named a sales award in his honor. Despite his work in the business world, he still looks back with special fondness on his naval years. His memory of those years, recorded here, will serve the interests of historians and others who want to learn more about the life of a destroyerman at war.

Special thanks go to Deborah Reid of the Naval Institute for his original transcription of the interview tapes and to Joanne Patmore of the oral history staff for the smooth typing of the final version. During the course of preparing the transcript for release, considerable editing was done in the interest of reducing repetition and putting material into chronological order. Some material was moved from one interview to another for the sake of continuity. Mr. Bak did both rewriting and editing of various portions of the transcript. For those scholars who are interested in seeing the original, unedited version of the transcript, it is on file at the Naval Institute.

                                              Paul Stillwell
                                              Director of Oral History
                                              U.S. Naval Institute
                                              March 1988

# Michael Bak, Jr.

| | |
|---|---|
| Education | Paterson State College, Paterson, New Jersey, 1946-1947 |
| 1948-1950 | Allied Stores Corporation executive training program under the GI Bill of Rights. Department store buyer at Quackenbush's Department Store, Paterson, New Jersey, responsible for buying stationery, greeting cards, typewriters, and candy. |
| 1950-1951 | Underwood Corporation, dealer sales representative covering the state of New Jersey. |
| 1951-1955 | Dealer sales representative covering Pennsylvania, Maryland, Washington, D.C., and New Jersey |
| 1955-1959 | Manager of Underwood's New York City office and dealer sales trainer. |
| 1959-1961 | Olivetti of Italy purchased the Underwood Corporation in November of 1959. Mr. Bak became the Manhattan sales manager for Olivetti Underwood Corporation. |
| 1961-1966 | National sales manager for consumer products (agent sales division). |
| 1966-1968 | Regional director of agents sales operation for the eastern region. |
| 1968-1970 | Corporate director of consumer products for the entire country. |
| 1970-1974 | Regional sales director again for the agent sales operation with headquarters in Michigan. |
| 1974-1977 | National sales manager of Franchised Business Products Division and responsible for organizing the sales and marketing programs for branch managers to handle dealer sales agents. |
| 1977-1979 | Regional director for the Eastern Region involved in sales to the Federal Government (Department of Defense) accounts. |

| | |
|---|---|
| 1979-1981 | Marketing manager for word processing at Olivetti headquarters marketing department. |
| 1981-1983 | Director of marketing programs for dealer operations. |
| 1984-1985 | Director of major market accounts and manager of all Department of Defense accounts east of the Mississippi. |
| 1985-1986 | Manager for Government/Education/Major Market Accounts (G.E.M.). |
| 1987-Present | National account executive for AT&T. |

On 12 March 1988, Mr. Bak was honored by the president of Olivetti USA for 38 years of outstanding sales achievement. A permanent plaque in his honor will be presented annually at the President's Club banquet to the outstanding Olivetti Sales Representative. The plaque reads "MICHAEL BAK, JR. AWARD OF EXCELLENCE FOR OUTSTANDING SALES ACHIEVEMENT."

Mike and Anne Bak celebrated their 40th wedding anniversary on 19 July 1987. They have three children, Bruce Michael, Kathleen Anne, and Randy Allen. They also have five grandchildren.

Authorization

The U.S. Naval Institute is hereby authorized to make available to individuals, libraries, and other repositories of its choosing the transcripts of oral history interviews concerning the life and career of the undersigned. The interviews were recorded on the 19 March 1984, 10 April 1984, and 11 June 1986, in collaboration with Paul Stillwell for the U.S. Naval Institute.

The undersigned does hereby release and assign to the U.S. Naval Institute all right, title, restriction, and interest in the interviews. The copyright in both the oral and transcribed versions shall be the sole property of the U.S. Naval Institute. The tape recordings of the interviews are and will remain the property of the U.S. Naval Institute.

Signed and sealed this _____ day of _____ 1988.

Michael Bak, Jr.

Interview Number 1 with Michael Bak, Jr.

Place: U.S. Naval Institute, Annapolis, Maryland

Date: Monday, 19 March 1984

Interviewer: Paul Stillwell

Q: Mr. Bak: Could you begin, please, by telling where and when you were born and something about your family?

Mr. Bak: I was born on March the 14th, 1923 in the city of Garfield, New Jersey.* Both my folks were immigrants from Russia.** My father settled in the United States in the latter part of the 1890s. Then my mother came over shortly thereafter, early 1900s. I lived in Garfield until I joined the Navy on December tenth, 1942.

Q: Did you live in the same house the whole time

Mr. Bak: We lived in the same house the entire time, yes.

Q: What business was your father in?

Mr. Bak: My father worked in a local woolen mill. He was in charge of the boilers and the engine room in the Samuel

---

*The U.S. national census reported the following population figures for Garfield: 1920, 19,381; 1930, 29,739; 1940, 28,044.
**The parents were Michael Bak, Sr., and Anna Bak (maiden name Chura).

Hird Company in Garfield, New Jersey.

Q: How long did he stay with that company

Mr. Bak: I believe he got his job around 1935, and he stayed with that company until he passed away at the age of 74. He worked for the entire time until his death. Only one Social Security check came. It had to be returned, because he died a few days before the check arrived.

Q: What are some of your recollections of your childhood--of going to school, play time, so forth?

Mr. Bak: In the early days it was kind of rough because my folks spoke Russian at home. While I was in grammar school, we spoke English. So it was a combination of coming back home and speaking one language, and in school, another language. My early upbringing was always with goals in mind, a close, goal-oriented family.

For recreation, my early years were spent in the local YMCA.* When I was seven years old, we were fortunate enough to live near a YMCA in Garfield. Most of my youth was spent at the "Y" in the evenings: playing basketball, learning how to swim, playing ping-pong, looking at magazines, and watching older boys and men playing basketball. At 12 years old I joined the Boy Scouts, a

---
*YMCA--Young Men's Christian Association

local troop (#4) in Garfield. Later, I joined another troop (#31), which was located in Passaic, New Jersey, and had a history of many Eagle Scouts. I was involved in camping and other scouting activities with the troop, such as lifesaving and work on merit badges. I remained with the troop until I joined the Navy.

In my high school years I played varsity baseball and varsity basketball. I was captain of the baseball team in my senior year. That was in 1941, the year I graduated and the year the war broke out with Japan.

Q: Did your parents eventually learn English?

Mr. Bak: Yes, they learned English the hard way. My father attended night school, in the same grammar school building that I attended. My mother didn't ever go to school. She was never able to read nor write. Yet she was able to do the things necessary to run a family.

Q: Was there an enclave of Russian-speaking people that enabled her to have some discourse and companionship?

Mr. Bak: Yes, in the area we lived in there was a Russian church that seemed to cater to the people who came over from Russia. It was a clannish type of thing where all our relatives and friends lived in the same area, within walking distance of each other. So we knew many people in the area that belonged to the same church.

Q: Have you retained your knowledge of the Russian language at all?

Mr. Bak: I speak Russian right now. However, I can neither read it nor write it. I can carry on a conversation in Russian and make myself known and get by without too much problem.

Q: Was there an active interest in, say, keeping in touch with people still in Russia, finding out how conditions were?

Mr. Bak: My father communicated with relatives in Russia. He would receive a letter probably once every three or four months from Russia. He also subscribed to a Russian newspaper called <u>Carpathian Russ</u> that gave him news of the back-home area.

Q: Was there any divided loyalty, or was he a wholehearted American?

Mr. Bak: He was a wholehearted American but kept his Russian heritage. In fact, he and my mother were very appreciative of all the benefits of living in this country. They had a very poor existence in Europe, and that was the reason why they both left. They eventually married and raised the five kids--three boys and two girls. The three boys served in the military. During the war, my older brother was in the Marine Corps, and my youngest brother served in the Navy after the war was over. He served aboard the USS Remey as a communications officer.*

Q: What part did religion play in the life of the family?

Mr. Bak: We were a very religious family. We went to church every Sunday as a family. That was also our social outlet, going to church and visiting relatives near the church. We'd either walk or take a bus to the church. But every Sunday it was duty in our family to go to church.

Q: Was this the Russian Orthodox faith?

Mr. Bak: Yes, Three Saints Church in Garfield, of the Russian Orthodox faith.

Q: What other outlets for recreation were there for you as a boy growing up?

Mr. Bak: The boys of our family were sports-oriented. We lived in a neighborhood with many boys who were always

---

*The USS Remey (DD-688) was a Fletcher-class destroyer, making her a sister ship of the USS Franks (DD-554), in which the interviewee served during World War II.

involved in playing baseball, basketball, and even football. We lived in a city that was known for champions in high school sports. When I was growing up, our high school had the best football team in the state of New Jersey for several years. So we always tried to emulate the different sports heroes in town. In fact, my folks sent me to Russian school located in the church hall, but I used to play hookey an awful lot to participate in sports. In the summer months, we swam often in a pond located one block from our home. I also learned to ice skate on the same pond in the wintertime. As a youngster I also started to save stamps. Some weekends were spent in a local one-room library.

My folks never did understand the reporting system that graded students in school. For example, if I brought a report card home and my mother would ask how I was doing, I'd say, "Mom, I'm the top student in the class," and show her the report card, which neither she nor my father could understand because of the language barrier. But I did pretty well in school. I was in the top 20% of my graduating class. I was also the first one in our family to graduate high school. Both my older brother and older sister did not graduate high school. They had to help make a living to support the family during the Depression years. It was very difficult.

In the late Thirties, my mother worked for the Forstman Woolen Company. She was spinning yarn in the woolen mills to make khaki uniforms. My youth was spent mainly having a good time--good, pleasant experiences, good neighbors, and ethnic people. We lived in a neighborhood of four ethnic types of people: an Italian neighborhood close by, a Polish and Slavic neighborhood close by, and a scattering of Russians in that particular area where I lived.

Q: Did you have an awareness of the Navy during your growing-up years?

Mr. Bak: Yes. Just by listening to the radio and reading local newspapers about Naval Academy activities. I was always interested in the sea. As a boy I used to read the Jack London stories.* I was very interested in his stories of the sea and going to the library and picking up different naval stories. I always felt if I ever got into the service, I would want to join the Navy.

Q: Just on the basis of this reading?

Mr. Bak: I was always impressed with the uniform, the reading, and I liked the excitement of possibly seeing the world. In fact, during high school days, a bunch of us fellows would take a bus into New York City and stand in Times Square and just observe all the people walking by.

---

*Jack London (1876-1916) was an American writer, author of such novels as The Call of the Wild (1903) and The Sea Wolf (1904).

You'd see a sailor with a New Zealand patch on his cap, or whatever country or whatever ship he was on. And we thought it was kind of salty, just seeing these sailors from various parts of the world. While growing up, even through high school, I never traveled beyond the borders of eastern Pennsylvania to the west, maybe southern Connecticut to the north, and Philadelphia to the south. I was never exposed to any other parts of the country until I joined the Navy. I did have the opportunity to win a baseball scholarship to the University of Roanoke. But in those days we had very little money to go to school further, and I never did follow it up. The offer was presented to me by a local alumnus of Roanoke University. His name was Peter Nicastro.

Q: Would it not have paid your whole way? Was that the problem?

Mr. Bak: It was not a full scholarship. I had to make a trip to Roanoke, and it was just quite a long distance away. Not having the finances to get there, I never did follow it up. One of my early regrets was not pursuing the offer.

Q: Did you ever contemplate going into professional sports? Was that an option?

Mr. Bak: Well, I always thought I could do pretty well in professional sports--in baseball primarily, not in basketball. I played American Legion baseball. I played high school baseball. I also played semipro baseball until the war came along and I joined the Navy. In fact, when I joined the Navy, I brought my baseball glove and ball with me. I had them with me for the entire time that I was on board ship. Whenever we docked anywhere, we would just throw a baseball back and forth on the docks.

Q: Did you follow the New York teams in baseball?

Mr. Bak: Yes. In those days we followed the New York Yankees and the New York Giants.

Q: So you probably got to the Polo Grounds and Yankee Stadium.

Mr. Bak: Got to the Polo Grounds and Yankee Stadium. In fact, in my early years the St. Louis Cardinals were also a favorite of mine because of Dizzy Dean and Paul Dean and the stories that were associated with them in the World Series of '34.*

Q: Did the Depression cause hardships in your family?

---

*J.H. "Dizzy" Dean and his younger brother, Paul "Daffy" Dean, were the pitching mainstays of the Gashouse Gang, the St. Louis Cardinal team which won the 1934 World Series from the Detroit Tigers.

Mr. Bak: Yes, we had a problem of gathering money. I peddled newspapers when I was a young boy. Made very little money. I also shined shoes, going from one tavern to another. My older brother was fortunate enough to work for a company known as the Manhattan Rubber Company. They gave him a job during the Depression because he was a good basketball player. My older sister eventually got a job as a waitress in a diner. My father was out of a job for quite some time during the early Depression years. At one time, if I recall, we were probably on subsistence with the local government, getting canned food and so forth. And my mother eventually got a job in the late Thirties. It was very tough. We had just enough food to exist. My mother did all the cooking, cooking the basic foods. They were foods that were very healthy, very inexpensive, and we rarely, rarely ever went out to dinner. I don't remember ever going to a restaurant until I was, maybe, late in high school years.

Q: There was not much chance for luxuries in that time.

Mr. Bak: There was no luxury at all. In fact, we just had the basic necessities in life. I never had a suit of clothes until I graduated high school. My first suit was a graduation present, 26 bucks.

Q: What subjects particularly interested you in high school?

Mr. Bak: I lived in a neighborhood that no one had ever completed high school, and I was the first to graduate high school in my whole area. And, as such, I took a business course, not figuring I would continue in college. In those years I wanted to be a court reporter, so I took shorthand and typing. I graduated with a commercial degree in high school.

Q: Did your parents provide any guidance on what sort of career you might go into?

Mr. Bak: None whatsoever. They had no knowledge of the careers that were open to the people of this country. Neither did our Russian relatives and friends. I was strictly on my own. In fact, I came home one time with my Boy Scout uniform, and one of our Russian relatives was visiting and berated my parents for allowing me to join the Boy Scouts. She felt there was a war coming on soon and that I would be the first one to be called up because of the uniform. It was the mentality in those days of those people--not in tune with what was going on in the educational world and not having the background. So one of the best things that happened to me from my standpoint was that my mother allowed me to do what I wanted to do. I never had any problems at home. As a result, why, we just happened to try to be aggressive and learn as much as we could in the various organizations that were available.

Q: Did your parents depend on you to keep them up to date on the culture in America since they had the language problem?

Mr. Bak: Well, they did, they did. But our entire family was helping in that respect: my oldest sister and my older brother and myself. My parents' needs were very simple. Their friends were church people. They basically were happy and content with their environment. They never complained about not having this and not having that.

Q: What means did you have for keeping up with the world around, current events and that sort of thing?

Mr. Bak: We eventually got a radio, and I was always reading papers. I used to deliver papers on Sundays, when I was eight or nine years old, for a local delivery man. In those days, they used to have a fellow coming down the street hawking papers and yelling out headlines of various national events. I remember when Lindbergh crossed the Atlantic Ocean, and he came down yelling, "Lindbergh crosses the Atlantic."* People would run out and buy a newspaper. Those were the only opportunities that we had.

Q: As the 1930s progressed, did it seem inevitable to you that you would get involved in a war?

Mr. Bak: Not in the beginning. When Germany was running unopposed through Europe, it started to sink in that we might someday be involved. However, I was also very fascinated by Hitler.* Every time there was anything written about Hitler, I always would read, because I always thought he was a madman and a jerk. Later on, I felt that we would be involved with a war. In fact, in North Jersey where I lived we had a city called Andover, which was known as a German bund camp, where young boys in brown shirts and brown pants would do their drills and so forth. Allowing young German-American boys to be trained in this country did not seem right to me. Being in high school, keeping up with world events was part of the requirement in courses, so I was well versed in what was going on in the world.

Q: What was the family's view of the Soviet regime in Russia?

Mr. Bak: Well, at that time not good. My parents had a

---
*Pilot Charles A. Lindbergh achieved the status of national hero in May 1927 when he flew from New York to Paris, the first solo flight across the Atlantic Ocean.
*Adolf Hitler became Chancellor of Germany in 1933.

very rough time, and I assumed they were persecuted in Russia. They had to get out, and that's why they migrated to America. I never once heard them say that, "I want to go back to live in the old country. I want to go back and carry the banner for Russia." They were very pleased to get out of there and create a new life in a country that had many opportunities, especially for the family.

Q: I wonder if there was any concern for relatives who were back living under that regime?

Mr. Bak: Well, that was always a concern. There were always problems going on. Whenever my father got a letter from the people in Russia, they were always writing about how bad conditions were and asking for money. The problem my folks had was the problem of survival and not being able to send money over. Never did my father or my mother ever say anything about, "I wish I could see the old town, my old country," like some people may have. They never did.

Q: A clean break.

Mr. Bak: A clean break, yes.

Q: After you were graduated in the spring of 1941, how did you spend the ensuing months before you went into the Navy?

Mr. Bak: That summer I was a counselor at a Boy Scout camp in Camp Aheka in Bear Mountains State Park, New York, located on Kanawaukee Lake

The four years prior to that, I used to work on a farm in the summer months. My older brother and I would pedal a bicycle to Richfield, New Jersey, and work on a farm. We used to pick tomatoes and do a lot of weeding, a lot of hoeing, doing farm labor from 7:00 o'clock in the morning until 6:00 o'clock at night with one hour for lunch. We would leave at 6:00 o'clock in the morning and ride a bicycle about 7 miles and 7 miles back.

In my junior year in high school, I was playing American Legion baseball, and I was ready to leave the team because I had to go to work and make some money for the family. But the coach had a connection with a company known as Gera Mills, a woolen mill, that allowed me to work from 4:00 to 11:00 in the evenings so I could play ball in the mornings all summer long.

Q: Did you contemplate getting some other, more permanent job after the camp counseling position?

Mr. Bak: Since I was pretty good in Gregg shorthand, and my typing skills were pretty good, I got a job in the Keller Engineering Company in Lyndhurst, New Jersey. They were looking for a male secretary; the men there didn't want any women in the company, because the language they used was sometimes kind of risque and rough.

Q: Did it turn out to be colorful, as advertised?

Mr. Bak: Yes, it was colorful. In fact, I'll never forget the expression the owner, Mr. Keller, used constantly when people would ask him if he was very happy. He said he was as happy as a dog in the forest full of tree, and a belly full of piss and six cocks to piss through. That's the kind of a thing that went on in the engineering company. It was a company that installed oil burners in homes that were being built.

Q: So you were mainly handling the correspondence?

Mr. Bak: Mainly handling calls, correspondence, and simple bookkeeping chores. After a while, they allowed me to drive a car to the sites to bring parts for different equipment they may have forgotten. I had a varied experience with the company. But primarily I was hired for my secretarial and business skills--at $16.00 a week.

Q: Was there an understanding that you would turn the income over to your family?

Mr. Bak: Well, we always did, even while working on the farm. It seemed to make my parents very happy, especially my mother. We were given an allowance.

Q: How long did that job last?

Mr. Bak: I was there about a year, and then I joined the Navy. One day I went to New York City and applied for the Navy.

Q: The Third Naval District headquarters was there, at 90 Church Street.

Mr. Bak: Ninety Church Street--that's where I went. When I received the official notice of acceptance, I was very happy. I was at work at the time, so my sister called and said, "Mike, your papers came in from the Navy. You're supposed to report to 90 Church Street on December the tenth."

Q: Did they do any in-processing there in New York--a physical or tests or what have you?

Mr. Bak: They had physicals there, yes. They did all of that. There was the routine of filling out papers and the routine of lowering your pants and coughing to make sure you had no problems--a basic physical.

Q: Where did you take the oath, in New York?

Mr. Bak: Yes. There was a roomful of young fellows. We took the oath there. Shortly thereafter, they put us on an overnight train. We didn't arrive in Chicago until the next day when the temperature was at about five degrees. I remember I had a high school varsity athletic jacket and no sweater underneath, just a shirt and a tie. In fact, the entire time we were in Great Lakes--it was from December through the end of March--in boot camp, I remember it was very, very cold.*

Q: Many people rushed right out and enlisted in December '41. Why did you delay a year?

Mr. Bak: Because I had a job earning money, had purchased a car, and because none of my friends rushed out to enlist. However, I did try to enlist in the U.S. Army Air Forces following an advertisement in the local papers. The prospect of learning to fly was exciting, so I wanted to join. The Air Forces had a tremendous drive on for pilots. I went to Newark, took my examinations, and flunked out. At that time, you had to have a college degree. If you had a degree, more than likely they took you in the Air Forces training program.

Then in our area there was talk about the draft. Nobody

---

*Recruit training, known more commonly as boot camp, was conducted at the Naval Training Center, Great Lakes, Illinois, about 30 miles north of downtown Chicago on the shore of Lake Michigan.

in my area went out and actually joined quickly. Everyone seemed to be waiting for the draft. I was one of the first ones in my whole area to enlist.

Q: What was your draft status?

Mr. Bak: I joined much before I would have been drafted. I put in for the Navy, and it was months before they actually accepted me. It was a period of time of waiting to get into the service. In the early part of '42, I also remember that it was tough getting into the United States Navy. Then, later on, it seemed to open up, and they were really after everybody to join.

Q: Did you have any ambition at all to go to the Naval Academy?

Mr. Bak: I did, but with my ethnic background and not knowing a lot of people in high places, I never felt I had an opportunity. I would have loved to attend Annapolis.

Q: Was there a general aura of patriotism among the people that lived in your area?

Mr. Bak: It was very patriotic. It was a feeling of togetherness that I never before witnessed in this country, nor will I ever see again. Every family had someone in the service, and everybody seemed to want to do their part. The folks from my side were producing the materials for the khaki uniforms. My father was working. My mother was working. My sister was working. My older brother joined the Marines. I was in the Navy. My younger brother was still in high school. He didn't get out until 1946. So he and my kid sister were the only ones at home. And then things were getting better financially for the family. I was sending money home that my sister was banking for me: an automatic shipment of $50.00 a month from my pay. So I had a nice substantial sum of money when I got out of the Navy.

Q: How thorough was the physical when you enlisted? Were they pretty strict about whom they would take?

Mr. Bak: It appeared to me they were very strict when I went through. I know some fellows who were in the line were not taken. I also remember them asking for my duty preference. I said destroyer duty, South Pacific.

Q: What was that based on?

Mr. Bak: The romance of the sea, movies that I had seen, and my readings of the excitement of destroyer duty. I think the key thing was being on a Navy ship and the ability to travel and see different parts of the world.

Q: How did your parents react when they found out you were enlisting?

Mr. Bak: They were supportive because of my enthusiasm and hoped that everything would go right. My parents always allowed me to make my own decisions, which I liked very much. I never gave them any trouble. So they allowed me to go with no problem whatsoever. They felt it was a duty. They were very patriotic from the standpoint of being foreign-born and appreciating what they had. So they were kind of happy to see that someone in our family was involved in the war effort.

Q: What experiences do you remember from boot camp when you got to Great Lakes?

Mr. Bak: It was a very busy place. I was put into Company 1895 with a chief petty officer in charge. His job was to whip the "boots" into shape, teach them seamanship, teach them regulations, and teach them the things they would need to know when they got aboard ship or further on in the Navy. The chief was Fred Lindstrom, who had been a professional baseball player by trade.*

Q: There was a man by that name who had been with the New York Giants.

Mr. Bak: That's what I think it was. He was a very intelligent man, very efficient, a person you were glad to be associated with. A person who had a good, positive outlook on life and would try to help you out without being a wise guy. I was very fortunate.

Q: How strict was the boot camp regimen?

Mr. Bak: It was very strict. They'd get us up in the middle of the night, and we'd start trudging through the snow at 2:00 o'clock in the morning. Later, when I was at sea and in general quarters situations, I realized then what they were doing at boot camp was putting you through the paces to make you feel like you would if you were aboard ship.

Boot camp was pretty nice in the sense that I played basketball and was put on the company team. As such, when

---

*Frederick C. Lindstrom (1905-1981) played major league baseball from 1924 to 1936 for the New York Giants, Pittsburgh Pirates, Chicago Cubs, and Brooklyn Dodgers. In 1924, at the age of 18, he established a record, which still stands, as the youngest player to appear in a World Series. Lindstrom was elected to baseball's hall of fame in 1976. After serving as manager of minor league teams, he was baseball coach at Northwestern University, Evanston, Illinois, and postmaster for that Chicago suburb.

the official duties were over, we would head over toward the gym and practice. We were involved in a league at Great lakes, where each company put together a basketball team. As a member of the team, I never did any mess cooking or cleaning up like the other recruits in our company did. We marched as a group to breakfast in the morning. We marched to lunch. We marched everywhere we went. We rarely were on our own, except when we were finished with our day's activity.

Q: Did you get liberty to go to Chicago at all?

Mr. Bak: Not too often. We used to get liberty every other weekend. I went to Chicago a few times, but we mostly went to Milwaukee. To me Chicago seemed unfriendly, probably because of not knowing much about the city. We found that Milwaukee was a city that was very friendly to sailors. I first herd of Masonry through the people there who opened up their lodge, and they provided us with food and good music and with dancing. We met some young ladies. One of the reasons I joined the Masonic Order years later was the fact that the people with the Milwaukee Masonic lodge opened up their hearts. They were very charitable.

I remember taking a train often from Great Lakes to Milwaukee. It was about an hour ride. When we got off the train, there would be a line of cars waiting at the curb. From the train station we would go downtown. These cars would be owned by very attractive young ladies who would watch sailors coming down the road. If they liked the looks of a particular sailor, they would invite him over and offer to take him out on the town. I was never fortunate in those days to have anybody pick me up. I had to do my own thing. But we would go from there to a USO, which was excellent.* They had a listing of things you could do for free in Milwaukee. For example, servicemen were able to ride streetcars without charge.

I visited many places in the United States during my Navy career, but I would say Milwaukee was the best city for liberty, because they were so friendly and so appreciative of servicemen. It just seemed that everybody in Milwaukee had somebody in the family who was a member of some service unit, and they wanted to reciprocate by making people welcome. We always went to the USO. That was the starting point.

Q: What kinds of things were available at the USO?

Mr. Bak: They had a nice place to read. There were quite a few free movies available at local theaters. If we liked a particular movie, free passes were provided by the USO. They would also have a list of families who would say, "If you have any GIs, we'd like to have them over for dinner."

---

*USO--United Services Organization--an outfit which provided recreational opportunities for servicemen away from home.

The USO would arrange to call the family, and we would go over and have a very nice home-cooked meal. From there we'd go back downtown and probably look for a place where they had dancing. And that was usually the Masonic lodge. Then we would sometimes stay overnight. We'd rent a room in the Hotel Schroeder. Get about six sailors from our company, with one fellow paying the bill and six of us sleeping all over the place, on the floor and in the chairs, and spend the night. Then in the afternoon on Sunday, head back towards the naval base.

Q: Was the discipline harsh for those who didn't make it back in time?

Mr. Bak: Yes, they had the discipline. But we rarely seemed to have the real problem fellows all during my career. I don't remember many guys getting in the brig. Maybe it was happening, but I didn't know anything about it.

Q: Did you have any buddies that you frequently went around with?

Mr. Bak: In boot camp, a fellow by the name of Bill Beckwith from Haverstraw, New York, was my closest friend. He and I used to go down on liberty most of the time together.

Q: What were the living conditions like in the barracks?

Mr. Bak: We slept in hammocks. We lived in a barracks that was a big open room with many stanchions to support the hammocks. Maybe the stanchion was about 3 inches thick, maybe 4-1/2 feet high. In the center of a square you would lash six different hammocks where six people would sleep in this group of stanchions. When you went to bed at night, you'd untie your hammock and spread it out. Then in the morning, when you got up, the first thing you had to do was resecure your hammock and lash it down. Every line had to be done just a certain way, so when you looked down the whole row, every one was in a uniform position. It was very regimented.

Q: Was it difficult learning to sleep in a hammock?

Mr. Bak: It was very difficult in the beginning. The barracks floor was made of a hardwood which had a very glossy, hard, shiny finish--very clean. You could hear all during our first night people falling right out of the hammock onto the floor. And you could hear some cursing going on from the sailors who fell. I fell one or two times my first night. But once we got the hang of sleeping in a hammock, then we never fell out again. During the entire boot camp training, which lasted about three months, we slept in hammocks.

Q: Did you carry that hammock with your sea bag when you were ordered to a ship?

Mr. Bak: No, no, that stayed with the training station. The only thing I carried with me was the sea bag, with my name stenciled on it. All my belongings that I was issued in boot camp were in there: basically whites and blues.

Q: And dungarees, I would imagine.

Mr. Bak: And dungarees and underclothes, and that was basically it. We carried our peacoat with us. One of the greatest pieces of clothing that I ever received in the Navy was a black woolen sweater with a high crew neck. And that was the warmest thing I ever had. I'd put that on over my T-shirt, and with the peacoat, no matter how cold it was outside, I always felt very comfortable, very warm. I had that sweater for many, many years until my teenage daughter confiscated it, and I've never seen it since.

Q: How was the food at boot camp?

Mr. Bak: The food at boot camp was very good. Coming from my background, where food was very scarce, I enjoyed every bit of my food. In fact, it reminded me of some of the Boy

Scout camps I went to. It was clean, wholesome food. It was neat. But a lot of sailors griped about the food. Maybe they had better food at home; I don't know. We had good Sunday meals. They tried to make it very pleasant for the "boots" in boot camp, I guess because they knew that we were going to be overseas soon.

Q: Were marching and drilling part of the regimen?

Mr. Bak: Yes, marching and drilling were constantly part of the regimen. In fact, we had daily training sessions of column right, column left, oblique march. Then we used to sing this song as we marched along to the tune of "Boogie-Woogie Hip Right, Hip Right." And then another song we used to sing going back and forth to chow line was, "Left, follow your left. Had a good job and we left." Just offhand, I don't remember any more.

Q: Did you develop a sense of camaraderie with your fellow "boots"?

Mr. Bak: Yes, it was a very close-knit group. I met for the first time fellows from different parts of the country. We formed the camaraderie, and most of the fellows I palled around with seemed to be the fellows who played high school basketball, baseball, or even football. Beckwith was a football star in Haverstraw high school.

Q: Was there physical training other than the basketball you participated in?

Mr. Bak: Yes. A lot of calisthenics and a lot of running on the drill field, and we had rifle practice. I remember one night getting up with snow around a foot deep and running across the drill field, hundreds of yards long and running and running and getting all wet and just coming back in an hour or so later, exhausted. Getting to bed one night and an hour later getting up and doing the same thing over. I guess those were the toughest times in boot camp. Getting up in the morning was also a little tough. The petty officer on duty would come by with a billy club and hit those stanchions, and they would ring out.

Q: How early?

Mr. Bak: If I recall, it was 5:30 in the morning. And breakfast was in shifts. Sometimes it was 6:30, and sometimes it was 7:30, depending on the shift. We had a company schedule that we would follow.

Q: Did you have to stand watches while at boot camp?

Mr. Bak: Yes, I did stand watches in the barracks, and

they had a regular schedule posted.

Q: Was there a sense of mental pressure on you--that there would be consequences if you didn't do things correctly?

Mr. Bak: Well, there was, but I'm a pressure-oriented guy and have been all my life, so it didn't bother me at all. I sort of enjoyed it. There was a lot of action, a lot of things happening at boot camp. I enjoyed it thoroughly.

Q: Was there any aspect of it that was geared to weeding out people who wouldn't be suitable for shipboard life?

Mr. Bak: None that I recall. It could have been without me knowing about it. The biggest concern each of us had was, "Where are we going to go from here?" They wouldn't tell us until we graduated from boot camp and got our seaman second class stripes. From that point on, we got our orders, and each of us was separated. I was sent to quartermaster school at Great Lakes for an additional three months, and others were sent to signal school, radio school, and yeoman school. Still others went to different naval stations throughout the United States.

Q: While you were still in the boot camp, what professional subjects did you study there? Did you go to fire fighting training, for example?

Mr. Bak: I don't remember. If we did, it didn't leave an impression on me. Ours was just basic training, following The Bluejackets' Manual.* It just seemed that the whole emphasis of boot camp was to whip you into shape physically, learn Navy procedure, and teach you to obey orders.

Q: Did you go to classes during the day?

Mr. Bak: Yes, different classes, such as seamanship. We were constantly busy going places. There was never a period of time that allowed you to sit down and do nothing.

Q: Was there any emphasis on being able to swim, since you were going to sea?

Mr. Bak: Yes, we had a swimming area where we were tested, but that thought never came up as far as an emphasis on it. I passed my swim test easily, so I don't recall that being a problem. It just seemed to me that everybody who joined the Navy knew how to swim. I found out later on it wasn't true.

---

*The Bluejackets' Manual, which has been published by the U.S. Naval Institute in various editions over the years, has long been considered the "bible" for U.S. Navy enlisted men. It is the basic textbook and reference volume on a wide variety of naval subjects.

Q: Indeed, it wasn't.

Was there a battery of tests to see what aptitudes you had that might suit you for various Navy jobs?

Mr. Bak: There were intelligence tests toward the latter part of the boot camp training. I don't recall what they were specifically, but I know they said to us, "Based on these tests, you will be assigned certain locations."

Q: Is that what led you to get to quartermaster school?

Mr. Bak: Yes. I didn't ask for quartermaster school. I was just going to go with whatever they assigned to me. I didn't know much about quartermasters at all up until that point.

Q: Did you get treated better in quartermaster school than in boot camp?

Mr. Bak: Well, there was not the regimentation or the crap that went with boot camp. It was a more casual, student-oriented type of an atmosphere, where we had classes all day long on the various subjects covering quartermaster duties. I know we had a lot of chart work. We had a lot of navigation, astronomy, and things to do with duties aboard ship.

Q: As part of this training, did you go out on any vessels at all?

Mr. Bak: No, there was no shipboard involvement whatsoever at Great Lakes. I was there from December tenth to the end of March, and there was no water. It was just frozen. It was so cold on the Great Lakes that we didn't use the ships for training.

Q: Was radar navigation any part of your training at that point?

Mr. Bak: No. If I recall, we did not have any radar training in quartermaster school. I myself was never involved with radar. Later on, at sea, the only people using the radar were the captain, officers of the deck, and the navigator.

Q Was there any signalman cross-training while you were at the quartermaster school?

Mr. Bak: Yes, we were given courses in both semaphore and the Morse code.* That was part of our basic requirement to be a third class quartermaster.

---
*The U.S. Navy employs three basic types of visual signaling: semaphore using a pair of flags at each end of the communication with different arm positions for the various letters; Morse code via flashing lights; and flaghoist which uses a colored flag to represent each letter and number.

Q: Did you have any carryover from your Boy Scout days on that?

Mr. Bak: Yes. When I was 12 years old, I was involved in semaphore signaling at Boy Scout rallies. We used to have troop rallies, where we had competitive teams in different Boy Scouting subjects. For example, we had a knot-tying team. We had a semaphore team. We had a bridge-building team, a pioneering team. I was involved in signaling in both Morse code and semaphore. So when I got to Great Lakes, the instructor, seeing that I knew semaphore, allowed me to take over instruction, while he just sort of observed and helped out the other people.

Q: What sort of textbooks did you have in quartermaster training? Did you use something like <u>Dutton's Navigation and Piloting</u>?

Mr. Bak: We used <u>Dutton's Navigation and Piloting</u>.

Q: <u>Knight's Modern Seamanship</u>?

Mr. Bak: I forget the exact name, but we did use textbooks, mostly dealing with navigation. We spent a lot of time with the navigational charts that we were going to use aboard ship--how to use them, how to keep them up to date. We also received in the mail notices to mariners that came out, I think, monthly. And in that we had to look for any corrections that had to be made to charts, so that we would have the latest markings on all buoys and channel markers.

Q: Was there a specific course book for quartermasters? Now they have correspondence courses that go with the ratings.

Mr. Bak: Every rating in the Navy had a basic book that listed all of the requirements for advancement. Ours, for example, dealt with hydrographic information, chronometers, compasses (magnetic and gyro), honors, rules to prevent collisions of vessels, and weather forecasting. Every pay grade in quartermaster had certain requirements to fulfill before you achieved that rate.

Q: What training did you get in the supervisory aspects of your job that you would have as a petty officer?

Mr. Bak: A general training course for petty officers third class. We were just drilled that our station was going to be the bridge, and we would be the assistant to the navigator and officer of the deck.

Q: Since you would be dealing with officers more than most ratings, was there any training on how to do that?

Mr. Bak: None that I recall. However, it seemed that the courses we took emphasized the fact that we would be on the bridge dealing with the officers daily. The more proficient you became, the better off you would be.

Q: Is there anything else about quartermaster school that sticks in your mind? Was there a lot of practice work? Did you take celestial sights?

Mr. Bak: No, we didn't take celestial sights at quartermaster school. We did talk about the sextant and its use, but it was difficult to take celestial sights on land. We spent most of our time learning how to work as assistants to the navigator. For example, taking time, identifying stars. We had courses in astronomy--what stars we were to use at sea for navigation purposes. We covered care of the bridge and charthouse. That is all that I can remember regarding quartermaster school.

Q: How did your assignment to the USS Franks come about?

Mr. Bak: I received instructions to be aboard a train going to Seattle, and I was told I was going to be going on board a ship known as the USS Franks, the DD-554, which was going to be commissioned in Bremerton, Washington.* We had to report to Bremerton by a certain day in July of 1943.

Q: When were you released from the school at Great Lakes?

Mr. Bak: I would say in early July. We got on board a train and probably got to Bremerton around July the tenth.

Q: She was commissioned on the 30th of July.

Mr. Bak: We were there several weeks before the commissioning to make sure the equipment was on board, all the gear that we would be using on the bridge.

Q: Was this ship essentially complete when you reported?

Mr. Bak: No, they had some work to be done yet. It wasn't until just before commissioning that the ship was completed. There was a lot of workmen on board ship, a lot of electrical lines over the sides.

Q: Did you move aboard the ship right away?

---

*The Franks, a destroyer of the Fletcher (DD-445) class, had been launched on 7 December 1942 by the Seattle-Tacoma Shipbuilding Corporation, Seattle, Washington. Fitting out and equipping were completed at the nearby Puget Sound Navy Yard, Bremerton, Washington.

Mr. Bak: No, I lived in a receiving ship with other crew members until the ship was completed. Later on, on board the _Franks_, I lived in a compartment amidships. The bunks were three tiers high. I had a lower bunk. It was a compartment with a lot of other sailors in it. Being a third class petty officer, why, I don't think I had any priorities. They just gave me that bunk. Radiomen, sonarmen, signalmen, and quartermasters all seemed to be in the same area that I was in.

Q: Did you have to pass a test to make third class?

Mr. Bak: Yes. We did that at Great Lakes.

Q: You were lucky going aboard ship as a petty officer then.

Mr. Bak: Yes, I was very lucky; I made more money.

Q: You also didn't have to put up with the dirty work that goes with being a nonrated man aboard ship.

Mr. Bak: That is true. However, aboard ship, we were still involved in chipping paint and using the steel wire brush to get the rust off. We had to constantly keep that bridge free of all rust spots and chip the paint. Everybody was responsible for his area of the ship. So that duty I had, but as far as anything like mess cook duty, I never had that all during my career in the Navy.

Q: Was it hard to adjust to this lack of privacy in the compartment?

Mr. Bak: Not to me, because as a young boy I belonged to the YMCA, and we were used to showering in a room together. When you're eight, nine, or ten years old, why, in the beginning you have a little fear of taking a shower with people around and being in close quarters to people, but it never bothered me after that. I didn't have the feeling of being cramped in the <u>Franks</u>. It was tight, but I adjusted and enjoyed it.

Q: Was there any grab-ass or horseplay among the sailors?

Mr. Bak: I have never seen that. I've heard the stories of dropping the soap.* I never saw anybody with a homosexual problem aboard our ship. We did have some sailors aboard our ship, on the California coast, who would spend their liberties rolling faggots in Los Angeles. I know one fellow in particular who used to go out and steal wristwatches off these guys, beat them up, and come back to the ship and brag about it. He would show wristwatches on

---

*One form of horseplay involved goosing a man in the rear end when he dropped his soap in the shower and leaned over to pick it up.

his arm and try to sell them. But that was the only instance I ever heard of or, it just seemed in those days that everybody kept to himself.

The only problem we had was kind of ridiculous. One of our guys complained one time to one of the guys that we had steaks too often aboard ship. There was always steak--steak every night. We were getting sick and tired of steaks. But that was in Southern California when we were just on that initial shakedown cruise. Later on, when we got to the South Pacific, we wished we had some of the good food. It got kind of rough as far as food went.

Q: Was the word put out on how you should or should not behave while on liberty?

Mr. Bak: Well, yes. They always made sure that when we left the ship, we looked shipshape--proud of your uniform and ship. We didn't want anybody looking disheveled. But as far as behavior itself, they more or less left it up to each individual sailor. On the ship I was on, it seemed like fellows got together in groups of five or six, and each group went their own way. I palled around with the same basic five or six guys during my entire career in the Navy.

Q: Was there any special emphasis to try to cut down on venereal disease?

Mr. Bak: Yes. In the early days of boot camp, we saw some pictures of what venereal disease can do to a penis; they were really disgustingly shocking. It just made you sick to think about having intercourse with a woman. That sort of discouraged you from womanizing or chasing broads.

After boot camp, I think, everybody was on their own; they're big boys. If you wanted prophylactics, the doctor had them available aboard ship and gave them to the crew members who wanted to use them. But I don't believe all the sailor stories I read about all these guys getting laid all the time and really shacking up. There may have been some of that going on, but not everybody was promiscuous. In wartime, in any liberty port, the ladies that may have been available could have been carriers of VD. Some of the sailors didn't care and took chances. Some of the women I've seen sailors with, the sailors would never have invited to their own homes. My God, they were ugly; they were dirty. I mean, Jesus. There were no beauties around that were available for the picking. There were so many sailors around and so few women that they all must have looked like queens.

Q: You wouldn't give them a second look back home.

Mr. Bak: Oh, my God, I've got a picture of one of them with one of the guys who will be at a reunion with me. I don't even want to show him the picture of him and that dog. In fact, as a young man, he wanted to marry one of the girls in Los Angeles. We prevented him from marrying her, because she was a run-around. She was a regular common whore. But the young kid fell in love. So maybe it was his first experience, I don't know. The only time we probably ever had the opportunity to have sex would be in Honolulu, number one. And the only other time would be in Japan when the war was over, because in between there was nothing.

Q: How were liberties in Seattle?

Mr. Bak: Liberties in Seattle were kind of difficult, because I didn't know anybody there. We used to take a ferryboat ride across the Puget Sound to get to Seattle. It took about an hour and a half on a boat called the Kalakala.* And most of the time going across Puget Sound was spent rolling dice, and sometimes you lost your money and you had to go back to the ship. When we'd get off the ferryboat in Seattle, we went downtown and went probably to a local tavern where sailors would hang out, or go to a movie, go to a park, look around. It was difficult to meet young ladies there, because they didn't have the openness that we saw in Milwaukee. There weren't as many

---

*For a history of the Kalakala, written by a World War II Navy enlisted man, see T.C. Mason, "The 'Flying Bird' of Puget Sound," U.S. Naval Institute Proceedings, January 1984, pages 62-68.

opportunities as in Milwaukee to enjoy ourselves, due probably to the greater number of sailors in the Seattle area. So we basically didn't do much in Seattle at all. We weren't there very long to do much. We didn't have liberty except maybe two or three weekends in Seattle. So we just more or less went sight-seeing.

Q: Did you go ashore at Bremerton at night?

Mr. Bak: Rarely. As far as I know, there was nothing in Bremerton other than loads of sailors. I never left the ship other than to go to Seattle. It just seemed that we didn't have much time at all, because we seemed to be busy aboard ship.

Q: Doing what kinds of things?

Mr. Bak: I suspect most of our time there was loading equipment, supplies, and ammunition.

Q: How much training went on during that period while you were still at Bremerton?

Mr. Bak: Very little before commissioning. Each section of the ship was involved in preparing its station for duty at sea. We had a chief quartermaster by the name of Justin

Grace who knew his way around the bridge. And he knew exactly what had to be done. I'd say he was a three- or four-hash mark chief quartermaster.* He had a lot of experience in the Navy. He was the one who was the mother hen to me, as a new quartermaster who had never been to sea before. He took me in the charthouse and showed me where all our gear was, where my station would be, and some of the things we'd be responsible for.** Without him I think I would have been lost as a quartermaster.

Q: Everybody has to be trained by someone.

Mr. Bak: We had another third class quartermaster aboard, a fellow by the name of Robert Kuhl. Then we had a striker, Richard Golter, a young boy that had never been to sea before.*** I guess he was a seaman first who was put in the quartermaster gang.****

Q: How much contact did you have with the officers in that

---

*A hash mark is a slanting strip of cloth worn on the lower left sleeve of an enlisted man's uniform to indicate the completion of four years of service. Thus, Chief Quartermaster Grace had at least 12 years in the Navy if he was wearing three hash marks and at least 16 if he was wearing four.
**The charthouse was a compartment just aft of the bridge. It had a chart table for plotting navigational positions. The charthouse also provided stowage space for charts and navigation publications carried by the ship.
***A striker is an enlisted man who has been designated to train for a particular rating but has not yet been advanced to petty officer in that rating.
****A "seaman first" was shorthand for "seaman first class," pay grade E-3, in the Navy of World War II. The lowest petty officer rate, third class, is E-4.

early period?

Mr. Bak: Everybody came to the bridge to congregate there and look around. I guess that was the focal point for the officers when they weren't down in the wardroom. So I knew them all by name in a short period of time.

Q: Was there a gulf between officers and enlisted in terms of familiarity?

Mr. Bak: Yes, definitely. They had a separate wardroom where they had their meals around a large table. And they kept to themselves more or less. They were very friendly on duty. But they palled around with themselves. It was clannish, definitely.

Q: How formal were things on the bridge?

Mr. Bak: It was very formal. Each officer of the deck was always trying to impress the captain that he was doing a good job, which most of them did. I thought it was a very first-class operation, being at sea for the first time and not having been involved with a ship, not involved with Navy protocol. I was impressed with the background of the people aboard the ship. We had quite a few experienced sailors and officers who had been to sea before--the gunnery officer, the navigator, the executive officer, Lieutenant Commander Millett.* And our captain seemed to be very knowledgeable of handling a ship.

Q: That was Commander Lidstone.

Mr. Bak: Lidstone, yes.**

Q: What impressions do you have of him?

Mr. Bak: Very professional, very intelligent, knew what he was doing, in command of the situation at all times. He seemed to really thoroughly enjoy being the commander of the ship.

Q: How could you tell that?

Mr. Bak: Well, just his mannerism, just by observing him in action. He enjoyed getting the ship away from the dock and getting out to sea. I don't know whether it was his first command or not, but he just seemed to be happy in command of that ship. It was a brand-new ship, new crew, the excitement going out to sea.

Q: Did he seem to have a good deal of self-confidence in

---
*Lieutenant Commander John R. Millett, USN.
**Commander Nicholas A. Lidstone, USN, was the first commanding officer of the Franks.

his ability to handle the ship?

Mr. Bak: Yes, I thought he had a lot of self-confidence. I thought he was very capable, very knowledgeable in all aspects of the ship. We were on a shakedown cruise, and this was my first experience at sea, so I was very impressionable about what was happening aboard ship. If they did anything wrong, I couldn't tell. But it was nice being on the bridge as a quartermaster, because that's where all the action was. If anything screwed up, you knew about it. You knew where the ship was going. You knew what the captain said. In fact, every time I came down to the chow line, the enlisted men would call me "wheels" because I was a quartermaster and they wanted to know what was going on, what was new.

Q: Did they try to pump you?

Mr. Bak: Always. Trying to know where we're going, what we're doing, what was said. I rarely gave out information about an officer. I just kept it to myself. I didn't want to be known as the fellow who was gossiping around and passing out rumors. I just fed them information I thought they would want to know that would not affect anybody up on the bridge.

Q: Did other ratings seem envious of this access you had

to the information?

Mr. Bak: No, I don't recall anybody seeming envious at all.

Q: Do you remember anything about the commissioning ceremony?

Mr. Bak: The *Franks* was placed in commission on Friday, July 30th. I remember a lot of speeches being made, a lot of people there. It didn't take very long, if I recall. The ceremony took place on the fantail. Since we had such a large crew, I did not have a good view of the ceremony.

Q: Did you feel fortunate to be going to a new ship?

Mr. Bak: Yes.

Q: Why?

Mr. Bak: She was part of the *Fletcher* class, and that was supposed to be the latest technology in the Navy. Everybody said, "Hey, you're on a *Fletcher*-class destroyer; that's great!" It was not a four-stacker or some of the older destroyers that were plodding the seas. We seemed to be getting the best there was. The sailors who had previous sea experience raved about this new type destroyer. My feeling about the ship was a carryover from their conversations.

Q: A lot of destroyer people have a great deal of affection for the Fletcher class.

Mr. Bak: I thought it was a great ship. What we went through, and how it withstood all the rigors of the sea, was amazing. It was still afloat when the war ended.

Q: After commissioning you moved out for shakedown. Was this a period of considerable training for the crew?

Mr. Bak: Yes, that was my first training period at sea and the first time for actually doing the things we'd learned in school. For example, leaving Bremerton I was on the pelorus stand for the entire nine or ten hours out the Puget Sound. We had a tube on the bridge next to the pelorus stand, where we would call out the tangents.*
The navigator was in the charthouse plotting the positions.

---

*The pelorus is a large metal ring equipped with either a telescope or other sighting device. It fits atop the circular gyrocompass repeater and can be rotated to measure compass bearings to objects ashore or other ships. In coastal piloting, the quartermasters take bearings to objects ashore or to the right of left side (tangent) of a body of land. Several bearings are taken almost simultaneously. When plotted on a chart by the navigator or quartermaster, the point at which the lines of bearing intersect provides a fix of the ship's position. When the ship is moving the bearings are taken frequently and the ship's position updated frequently.

Bak #1 - 50

Q: Did the chief teach you how to take bearings and so forth?

Mr. Bak: I knew how to take bearings, because we learned it in school. I knew compass from my Boy Scout days. I was very familiar with compass bearings. I knew the charts. I knew where the markings were. The chief would point out, "These are the things we want to look for when we're coming out. There will be a smokestack here or be a building here, or an island here on the left tangent or the right tangent." I would yell these bearings out, and the navigator would be plotting these points on the chart.

Q: Sometimes it gets foggy up in that area. Did you have any low-visibility piloting?

Mr. Bak: The first time out, no. We had no problems with fog or visibility at all. It was a clear day when we left Bremerton, and it was an all-day ride. Among other things, we were testing the engines, the maneuverability of the ship.

Q: Where did you go from there?

Mr. Bak: We went out to the Pacific, and then we headed down towards San Diego, where we were taking the ship for the shakedown cruise. However, before we left for San Diego we had completed receiving torpedoes, depth charges, and ammunition.

Q: What kinds of training did you get during the shakedown?

Mr. Bak: Gunnery exercises--test firing structural test shots from all 5-inch guns, 20-millimeter and 40-millimeter guns. We were also checking to see that the magnetic compasses were working properly and calibrating the direction finder.

Q: Did you go through any general drills--man overboard, abandon ship, general quarters?

Mr. Bak: Yes, aircraft from San Point Air Station made drill dive-bombing and torpedo attacks on our ships.* We also had fire drills and exercised at collision drills and steering casualty drills, and the ship held dawn general quarters every morning. Man-overboard drills were also included. I particularly recall the bang of the alarm: "General quarters, man your battle stations." The captain would call it at random. He would call it at nighttime and get us out of bed. That's when we would complain about the horseshit that was going on with getting out of bed, not

---
*Sand Point Naval Air Station, Seattle, Washington.

realizing why and what we were in for. The first three or four days, leaving Puget Sound, most of us, including myself, were seasick. I don't think we could have done much anyway.

The basic goal was to get that ship down to San Diego and then join the fleet there and go through various shakedown exercises. I remember that we fired our 5-inch guns at target sleds which were attached to a utility ship by means of a long cable and towed in the water. We had submarines in the area that we would work with, and then also we would bombard the island of San Clemente with our 5-inch guns. We fired the 5-inch guns, the 40-millimeter guns, and the 20-millimeter guns at the airplane sleeves. At times we would get a report back that we just missed the airplane. We'd catch hell from the pilot.

Q: Understandably so.

Mr. Bak: Yes.

Q: What was your battle station?

Mr. Bak: My battle station was constantly the bridge, assistant to the navigator and the officer of the deck.

Q: What kinds of things would you do at general quarters?

Mr. Bak: Well, I would be involved in providing the navigator with any of the navigation equipment and aids. Making sure the binoculars were available. Just making myself available at the beck and call of the officer of the deck, the navigator, or the captain. Sometimes we'd take the wheel during general quarters.

Q: Did you get instruction about keeping the quartermaster log?

Mr. Bak: Yes, that's one of the most important duties that we had. The log was a green-colored ledger-type book. We posted different things that happened aboard ship such as: date and time we got under way, changes in course and speeds, changing of the watch, who's on duty and anything that may have occurred during passage. We would also enter the fleet organization that we were attached to, for example, Destroyer Division 94 operating under ComThirdFlt on temporary duty with TF 39, (CTF39, Rear Admiral R.W. Hayler, USN, ComCruDiv12, USS Montpelier, flagship), as well as the zone time.

We also entered the time we commenced firing during gunnery practice. We would also enter time the other ships in the formation commenced firing. If we were firing at enemy shore batteries we would enter the time, results and number of rounds each gun class expended. When three of our crew received medals from the captain for heroism, their names, rank were also entered. When we crossed the equator, we posted the fact that we initiated crew members upon their first crossing. When we took on fuel, we reported the number of gallons received as well as the refueling ship. When we picked up a pilot out of the water, we entered the name, rank, and the carrier that he was attached to. Whenever we loaded ammunition, we would enter the number of rounds for each class of gun. Whenever we received mail from a ship at sea, we posted the time and the ship's name. If anyone was hurt during battle, it was reported in the log. When enemy aircraft was reported in the vicinity, we noted the time and action taken. If we splashed a Jap plane, that was noted.

When we pulled alongside a nest of destroyers at anchor, we would list the ships' names. If we were at anchor, we would list the anchorage number assigned to us. When we were anchored with the rest of the fleet in a lagoon, we would list the senior officer present. Every time we were at general quarters, we entered the time and the time we secured. In port or at anchor, we listed new crew members reporting for duty. We also reported transfers. We entered navigational reports three times a day. When the boilers were lit, the time was reported. When we received an action report from the admiral, it was reported in the log. The first class yeoman used the quartermaster's log to type the daily war diary of our ship. The officer of the deck would then sign his name to the official war diary, attesting to the correctness of the activities during his watch.

Q: What about working with other ships during that shakedown period? Did you get an opportunity for that?

Mr. Bak: Yes, we worked with other destroyers, with destroyer escorts, and submarines.

Q: What was the emphasis on during that period-- antisubmarine warfare or antiaircraft, or just what?

Mr. Bak: Both. One was submarines--they would have a submarine in the area that would descend to give our sonarmen the experience of having a real submarine in their sounding gear. We spent several weeks just doing that, and we had an awful lot of practice with shooting at air and surface targets. We would visit various offshore areas at San Clemente island that we used for bombardment purposes. We would pick targerts on the island and, using tangents and navigation, pinpoint certain areas that were targets on the beach.

Q: That certainly called your people into play on the navigation.

Mr. Bak: Yes. In fact, if I recall, they had somebody on

land tracking down the accuracy of the shots.

Q: A shore fire control party.

Mr. Bak: A fire control party--that's what it was probably called, yes. They would say, "Up 400, down 500, left 500, on target, keep shooting."*

Q: Did you get a little tired of hearing those guns going off constantly?

Mr. Bak: Yes, it was one of the things that was really tough. The 5-inch guns made a tremendous noise, especially when they all went off at the same time. The hospital corpsman went around the entire ship with a lot of cotton. We'd jam it into our ears every time we had firings.

Q: Did you find that you were enjoying the life at sea as you got into it?

Mr. Bak: Once I got over my seasickness the first several days, I enjoyed it thoroughly, because we were doing a lot of things that I'd heard about, but was never involved in.

---

*By voice radio, the shore fire control party gave the ship corrections as a result of spotting the fall of shot. These corrections were then fed into the ship's fire control equipment to improve the accuracy of succeeding rounds of fire.

We were working with several ships in a destroyer division, working as a team together in maneuvers. I think we used every part of the ship at one time or another during the shakedown cruise that would finally allow us to leave for the war zone with the understanding and knowledge that we were prepared to do battle if and when the time came.

Q: Was there a sense of excitement to all this?

Mr. Bak: Yes, because I would say 85% of the crew was never at sea before. Maybe that's high. But it just seemed that most were raw recruits doing for the first time things they had been taught. It was excitement, because it was where all the action was at. It was nice.

Q: Was there a sense of urgency to get you out to the war zone?

Mr. Bak: I imagine there was because of the need for ships in the South Pacific, but the urgency I experienced was that of getting the ship in shape, and making sure that everybody was doing the things they were supposed to do.

Q: Did you have any sense of concern for your personal safety--that you were going into a pretty hazardous thing?

Mr. Bak: No, I never did and I don't know why. Maybe I was foolish enough and being young--20 years old--that I didn't think of those things. We left the States for Pearl Harbor. We knew it was the last day we'd see the States for a long time. But I always knew I'd be back sooner or later--just a matter of time. In six months we'd wipe the Japs off the face of the earth and we'd be back home. I mean, it was a we-couldn't-lose situation. And most of the friends I was with aboard ship had the same feeling. It was just a good, happy feeling. It was like a picnic, going to the war, you know, raising the flag. That's my impression of the thing.

Q: You mentioned the gambling had taken place on the <u>Kalakala</u>. Was that also on board the <u>Franks</u>?

Mr. Bak: Aboard the <u>Franks</u> we played cards more often than gambling, but we also gambled down below without any officers around.

Q: Did you have to post lookouts or something

Mr. Bak: Yes. I don't recall how we did, but we did gamble. The officers never bothered you at sea. I think if they did find out about it, they weren't that chicken-shit to put us on report. It just seemed like everybody was doing his own thing without getting anybody involved in problems. One day I won about 345 bucks in a card game, and when we had that accident while at sea and hit the New Jersey, I thought we were going down.* All I kept thinking of was 345 bucks in my locker down below. I was kind of worried about losing that.

Q: You had only a small locker. Was that inconvenient as a place to live out of?

Mr. Bak: Well, it was very small. I would say it was about 24 inches by 24, maybe 12 inches high. It housed all our gear, but it took every bit of space to house all our gear. We used to have locker inspections to make sure that some of the fellows didn't have things in their locker that weren't supposed to be there. You'd stand by your locker, and as the officers came by, they would ask you to open your locker up right in front of them, take everything out, look inside. Maybe somebody was missing something. Maybe there was a pair of binoculars gone.

Q: Another big no-no was having somebody else's clothing in your possession.

Mr. Bak: Yes, that was a no-no.

---

*On the night of 2 April 1945, while operating off the coast of Okinawa, the Franks was damaged as a result of colliding with the battleship New Jersey (BB-62). Mr. Bak discusses the collision in detail later in the oral history.

Q: Were there any cases of thievery in the compartments?

Mr. Bak: My recollection is that I left my locker open a lot of times, stuff on my bunk. When I took a shower and came back, it was always there. For some reason, we never seemed to have that problem.

Q: Were there any other forms of recreation while you were under way? Did you have movies?

Mr. Bak: There was no place to hold a movie under way. The only time we ever had movies was at an anchorage, where we would have the fantail rigged up with a screen.

Q: What off-duty outlets did you have on board ship?

Mr. Bak: Not a hell of a lot. When guys were off duty, they usually went to the location where their duty station was. For example, I was often on the bridge. If I wasn't on duty, I was with the signal gang, sitting on a flag bag, or in the charthouse cleaning my station. I would say the biggest recreation we had was just shooting the breeze in the station that you were located in, or we might be reading or resting in our sacks.

Q: What kinds of things would you talk about?

Mr. Bak: I guess girls, things you did back home, family, the past liberty, where we're going. For example, when we were going to Honolulu, we would try to get some guys who had been there to talk about their experiences. What could we expect? But the basic conversation was about home, family, relatives, girlfriends, husbands, wives, kids, sports interests.

Q: Was there any desire to be back home? Was that included in this discussion?

Mr. Bak: Yes, some people had a desire to be back home. But I think the majority of our shipmates, in the beginning, were anxious to go see new parts of the world like I was. I think the only time I really thought of being back home was when I saw the Liscome Bay go down, and then I realized the war was on, and we're going to have some people not making it back home.* But up until that time, everybody thought it was just a matter of, "Well, we've got them beat. We'll do the job and come right back home with no loss of lives or anything."

Q: What part did mail play in your life on board ship?

---

*On 23 November 1943, the escort carrier Liscome Bay (CVE-56) was torpedoed and sunk by the Japanese submarine I-175. Of her complement of some 900 officers and men, fewer than 300 were rescued.

Mr. Bak: Mail was a very big part with my life and everybody else's life, because that was the only communication we had on what was going on back home. And although I was never a big letter writer, I enjoyed getting mail more so than actually sending mail.

Q: That's the way with most people.

Mr. Bak: Yes. With the large family that I had back home, I was fortunate in getting a lot of mail. I had a sister that wrote regularly. Then, later on, I started writing regularly to her. Plus, we had some neighbors that took it upon themselves to keep people posted on what was going on back home. Mail call was a very, very big part of the whole thing.

Q: Was your sister the link with your parents?

Mr. Bak: My older sister kept them posted on what was going on in my life in the military. They knew why I was there, but they had no knowledge of a Navy ship. I don't believe they had ever seen a Navy ship. From San Diego I sent them a picture of the <u>Franks</u>, which my mother had posted in the house. But my sister was the focal point for all communications between myself and my family.

Bak #1 - 63

Q: Was the mail pretty tightly censored on what you could and couldn't say?

Mr. Bak: Yes, every bit of mail that we had had to be read by an officer. They had a round marking censor stamp, and the officer would sign his name or initials in the censor circle.

Q: What kinds of things couldn't you talk about?

Mr. Bak: Where you were going. What type of training you were involved in. What you were actually doing. What you were shooting. What kind of guns we had. All I wrote home about was things are going very well, positive attitude, enjoying myself, food is good or food is lousy, had some great sea duty, or liberty in California, went to certain places in Hollywood, Los Angeles, and Mexico.

Q: What were some of those liberties like in Southern California?

Mr. Bak: We did go to the Palladium a few times in Hollywood, a dance place that catered to servicemen. It was an area where a lot of ladies visited also and met servicemen. You could always find a dancing partner. But I would say that most of the liberty that I had in California was primarily sight-seeing to visit different locations.

I didn't know anyone in California at all. A friend of mine, Charlie Lewis, who was a signalman, had an aunt and uncle living outside Los Angeles. I spent a few visits overnight with his family. We spent hours talking with them. They would take us around Los Angeles, to different museums and whatnot. Charlie was the only one that I knew who had any family in the area. He eventually became a pilot. He and I both took our exams on the aircraft carrier USS Hancock. They had a complement of so many Navy personnel to go back to preflight school in the V-5 program.* We both passed the exam. He eventually went back and became a pilot. Since I was a quartermaster first class at that time, they had nobody to replace my rating. As a result, I never did get back to go to school. That was my greatest disappointment in my entire stay in the Navy. I wrote back home and told them that I was accepted for preflight school and that I would be reporting to San Francisco. And they were excited for me, but I never did make it, as the captain wouldn't let me off. That was Stephan; he refused to allow me off the ship.**

---

*The exam Mr. Bak mentions here is one he took late in the war. The V-5 program trained naval aviation cadets to become pilots and officers. Those who successfully completed the training course were commissioned as Naval Reserve ensigns.
**Commander David R. Stephan, USN, was commanding officer of the Franks from 30 June 1944 until he was fatally injured on 2 April 1945 in the destroyer's collision with the USS New Jersey (BB-62).

Bak #1 - 65

Q: Did you have any dates while you were down there in Southern California?

Mr. Bak: Maybe one or two. That was a chance happening, nothing big. I met a gal at a dance place, probably took her to a movie, and that was about it. We never had time to do much of anything. Our liberties were short, and distances were great.

Q: Did you have a girl back home at all?

Mr. Bak: I had some girls back home. But when I left home, I told everybody that, "I don't know when I am coming back. Don't wait for me or anything like that." I did have a girl in high school when I graduated, lovely girl. But I left no ties back home at all when I left. So that way I didn't have anything to worry about, no "Dear John" letters. I was very anxious to go out there and see other parts of the world, not tied down seriously to anybody.

Q: Were you able to get enough sleep on board the ship?

Mr. Bak: In the beginning we had a lot of general quarters drills during the shakedown cruise. They did that, I guess, to let us know what we would be getting involved in later on in actual combat. Every sea detail, going in or out of port, I was on duty. I was on duty before the ship took off, getting everything ready for the bridge, and I was on duty after the ship pulled in, securing everything. So when everybody went on liberty when the ship pulled in, we had maybe 50 or 60 sailors all in their dress blues or dress whites ready to go over on land and start liberty, I was still on the bridge. If we were going out to sea and I had special sea detail, my watch may have started as soon as I finished the bridge detail. For example, going out the Puget Sound, I spent eight or nine hours on the bridge. It's possible I could have started my four-hour watch right after my special sea detail.

I know a lot of my gunnery mates aboard ship would be off duty and sleep in the gun mount when no action was going on, even during general quarters.

Q: That wasn't one of your options.

Mr. Bak: Was no option. Occasionally, if I was off duty and wanted to take a little nap, I would just jump into the flag bag, and pull the flags aside, and just go down there. It was musty sometimes with the flags, but that was the only place we had a chance to sack out, other than being in your bunk.

Q: Some people in certain ships would be too hot below decks and would sleep up on deck. Did you do that?

Mr. Bak: Very hot. yes, we slept on deck sometimes at anchor. But the problem with sleeping on deck at sea--if the water is rough, you have the problem of rolling and pitching, so you had to be down below for safety reasons. Besides, it's no fun sleeping on a steel deck.

Q: You could also get rained on.

Mr. Bak: And rained on, too. That was a tough one. That was a tough one.

Q: I would think that would be easier on a bigger ship where it's more stable.

Mr. Bak: Yes, I didn't see many fellows sleeping on the deck itself on our ship. They might have been on the torpedo deck, but not too often.

Q: Was there a big emphasis on darken ship and not shining any lights at night?

Mr. Bak: Yes, except during the time when we came back from Japan and went home, we had no lights. After sunset, the smoking lamp was always out. We had to maneuver back and forth to our stations in total darkness. Many times it was pitch black. You couldn't see anything. Lights were forbidden, and the crew really stuck by no lights aboard ship because of the possibility of being seen at sea. That was a problem. The other problem we had--we used to blow off smoke at nighttime in order to get the boilers free of the soot. You'd be topside, and sometimes that thing was blowing, so you'd get full of soot. But we only did that at nighttime and not during the day, because it would leave a trail.

Q: Did you have to go to the bridge early in normal underway watches to get your eyes night adapted?

Mr. Bak: Not necessarily. Usually I would be on the bridge early, visiting with the signal gang before going on watch. We did have on the bridge binoculars with infrared lamps on them. If it was pitch black and we were at sea, we used to stand on the signal bridge looking down at sailors walking along in darkness. We could see them, but they couldn't see us. That was a game we used to play, watching these sailors walk. We used those binoculars primarily for night signaling when they put a red sleeve over the signal light. We used those binoculars to keep an eye on the admiral's ship to see if there were any messages coming across in infrared light.

There was an expression we used to use: "You can always tell a destroyer sailor by the black marks on his ankles." The reason is that he'd bumped into a hatch that was sticking up above the deck and hit it in darkness.

Q: Was smoking pretty common?

Mr. Bak: I would say that 85% of the guys smoked aboard ship. I started smoking when I was about 21 years old. I was sitting in a gun mount, watching a movie in the South Pacific. I don't remember the island, but I was with a bunch of guys who were smoking in front of me. They offered me a cigarette and I stupidly took it, so I smoked for a number of years.

Q: At that time there wasn't nearly the emphasis there is now of the health hazard, was there?

Mr. Bak: None. I guess the biggest vices we had aboard ship were drinking an awful lot of coffee and smoking cigarettes. It just seemed that every station on board ship had a "joe pot" available for the crew members. That was a big thing.

Q: It was a way of life.

Mr. Bak: It was a way of life.

Q: Did you stand lookout watches at all?

Mr. Bak: Not actual lookout watches. As a quartermaster,

I could roam the bridge and do a lot of things. And I kept my eyes open. Mine would just be an overall lookout without any specific area to watch for.

Q: After your shakedown period, then you went back up to Bremerton for another yard period. What do you recall of that?

Mr. Bak: Well, I recall a lot of the yard workmen coming back on board and repairing things that might have gone wrong or some of the equipment that needed attending to.

Q: What was the shipboard attitude toward yard workers?

Mr. Bak: They were part of getting the ship together and repairing what had to be repaired. But I myself didn't have any feelings toward yard people at all, negative or positive. They were doing their job, like we sailors were doing our job.

Q: So there was no sense of resentment that they weren't part of the military?

Mr. Bak: No, not from my standpoint or anyone I knew of on the bridge gang or the guys I palled around with. Most of the yard workers looked much older.

Q: Cumshaw means paying off a guy with a can of coffee or sugar or whatever to get a particular job done. Was that part of your way of doing business to get supplies and equipment in the shipyard?

Mr. Bak: Not on the bridge. I never had that experience, nor did I know of anybody that had that experience. Maybe the gunnery people or the boatswain's people needed something done. But it just seemed that the bridge itself--it was always priority where the repairs were there, or the radar had to be repaired. The urgency was always there.

Q: Was keeping charts up to date part of your job?

Mr. Bak: Yes, that was part of my job.

Q: How much time did that occupy?

Mr. Bak: Well, it depended on the notices to mariners. We would correct charts basically in only the area of the world we were going through. For example, if we were going to Honolulu, we'd pull the charts out on all the Hawaiian Islands and make the changes for all the Hawaiian Islands, so in case we ever used those charts we were up to date. Then if we were going down to the Solomon Islands or Tarawa in the Gilbert Islands, we would pull those charts out that would reflect that area.

Q: Was there any concern about letting you know where you were going--that this might spread rumors or be a breach of security?

Mr. Bak: Yes, but actually no one knew where we were going except probably the captain and the executive officer. Whenever we pulled out of a port, no one in the crew knew where we were going until we were under way and out at sea, and then the captain would announce our destination.

Q: Wasn't there a tipoff, though, in what charts you would be working on?

Mr. Bak: I would probably know a day or two before the other crew knew. We would have a good tipoff when we got the charts out, and the announcement wouldn't be made until a day or two later.

Q: What about the navigator? Do you have any specific memories of him?

Mr. Bak: Yes, his name was Lieutenant (j.g.) David Forer, and I liked him. I thought he was an excellent navigator. He knew his stuff. He never seemed to be unsure of himself.

Q: Did he treat quartermasters with respect?

Mr. Bak: Yes, we had a very good relationship. I would take sights with him in the morning and the evening, as well as the sun line at noontime. My function with him was primarily in the morning to let him know where the stars were going to be setting up. Then I would tell him the time each star was measured, and he would lay out the triangle on the chart. I put his position report in the quartermaster log.

Q: How accurate were you able to be in your navigation?

Mr. Bak: Well, I would say extremely accurate. We would get a triangle of maybe a quarter of an inch to a half inch, and the position would be in the center of a triangle. He was very good.

Q: How useful was Loran in your long transits?

Mr. Bak: I went to Loran school in Honolulu, after we returned from being at sea for quite a while.* I would

---

*Loran is an acronym for long-range radio aid to navigation. It is based on the transmission of electronic pulses from stations on land. Shipboard equipment is used to measure the time difference between pulses and thus to establish lines of position on charts. The intersection of lines of position provides an approximate fix of the ship's position.

say it was in the middle part of the war when Loran became popular. I don't think we used Loran too extensively. We relied primarily on our celestial navigation.

Most of the time we were with a formation of ships. It could have been 30 destroyers in an outside screening circle with battleships and carriers inside the screen, so everybody was making their own navigational position reports. But we still took sights every day. Sometimes we were off by ourselves to do certain things where we'd have to rely on our own position reports. Sometimes we bombarded an island by ourselves. We'd take off and steam all night and get to the exact island just perfectly, right on target and then unload our 5-inch guns--maybe hit a radio tower on the land and then take off immediately. I don't recall ever that we were screwed up from a standpoint of not being in the right position. We always seemed to be--that's where the island is going to appear. If we were approaching Honolulu, we just expected to see on that particular bearing a mountain somewhere soon. And all of a sudden, someone would yell, "Land ho!" And it would be right there.

I don't recall Forer ever being screwed up as far as the navigation went. Very calm guy, very professional, and not an extrovert. I would say he was more of an introvert. He was also an artist. In fact, he is the one who designed that "home of the happy _Franks_" certificate that we gave the pilots when they crash-landed and we would pick them up. As a pilot was sent back to his carrier, he would receive a certificate announcing that he was picked up by the Franks, exact longitude, latitude, time, and the date, as a souvenir.

Q: Did you have any special training or practice in this plane guard role while you were in your shakedown period--how to recover men?

Mr. Bak: We didn't practice plane guard duties during our shakedown cruise off the California coast. We started operating with aircraft carriers shortly after entering Pearl Harbor. Training exercises with the carriers were held at every opportunity. During this period, we were involved primarily in screening the carriers. When we left for the Gilberts operation, the fleet held flight operations daily, provided the weather was good. It was this period of time that the Franks started plane guard duties. To me, it was on-the-job training. When the signal for commencing flight operations was hoisted, the Franks left her screen position and maneuvered behind the aircraft carriers assuming the role of plane guard ship. When the pilots were safely airborne, we returned to our position in the screen. When flight operations were completed and the pilots returned to the carriers, we again assumed our station as a plane guard ship.

If a plane went into the water, the captain would

maneuver as close as possible to the downed pilot, lower our whaleboat and attempt the rescue. Although we rescued a number of pilots using this procedure during Captain Lidstone's tour of duty, our technique was changed when Captain Stephan came aboard. He felt that the whaleboat technique was dangerous, especially in very rough weather. Besides, it took too long to get to the pilot. Instead, he had three swimmers available to attempt a rescue. These swimmers were equipped with a leather harness-type belt strapped to their waist. At the back of the belt a line was fastened to a secured eye ring. The swimmer would then dive into the water and swim towards the pilot. When the swimmer got to the pilot, he would grip an arm around him and signal for the men on the deck to pull him back to the ship. The special harness was designed by a second class boatswain's mate named John Ford.

Q: Was the harness connected to the life jacket?

Mr. Bak: No, the life jacket was separate. The harness was strapped to the waist. It was made of leather, about 6 inches wide, and strapped around the pilot's belly.

Q: What was the purpose of going to Hawaii?

Mr. Bak: We went out there to join the fleet and for further gunnery practice outside of Pearl Harbor while waiting for the invasion of Tarawa to take place. During this period, we also maneuvered with aircraft carriers. This was our first taste of plane guard duty.

Q: Did you know then where you would be going?

Mr. Bak: No. When we left Pearl Harbor, we had no idea until we were at sea, I think, a couple of days. Then the captain announced we were going to the invasion of Tarawa. He used the microphone to give the crew a capsule description of what was going to be happening and what we could expect. He stressed the importance of lookouts watching for enemy planes and watching for submarines, and basically being alert and also making sure that no lights are visible at nighttime.

Q: Was he liked and respected by the crew?

Mr. Bak: Commander Lidstone was very well liked and very well respected. He kept very much to himself but had a good rapport with the officers. He was not a fellow that would be congenial with the crew, not someone who would say, "Hi, Charlie, how's it going, what's new?" He was not a guy that was a glad-hand, an easy guy to be mixing with the crew. He was, however, friendly with the bridge crew.

Q: I think that is a role for the captain, to be isolated.

Mr. Bak: That's right. That's the role, and he played the role well, in my opinion.

Q: What were some of the experiences you had ashore in Pearl Harbor?

Mr. Bak: I immediately went to the Iolani Palace.* I had a cousin by the name of Daniel Serafin who had been stationed in Oahu since prior to the war. As a youngster in high school, I used to correspond with him, and the last known address I had was the Iolani Palace. So when I got to Honolulu, I jumped in a cab with a fellow by the name of Sigismund F. Kateusz, one of our signalmen. I asked the cab to take us to the Iolani Palace. When I got there, I found a sergeant sitting at a desk, and I told him I was looking for a cousin of mine named Daniel Serafin. Without blinking an eyelash, he made a telephone call within a minute. He gave me the telephone and said, "Here."

I said, "Danny?"

He said, "Yes, who's this?"

I said, "Your cousin Mike." He couldn't believe it.

He said, "Where are you at?"

And I told him, "The Iolani Palace."

He said, "Stay there. I'll pick you up in half an

---

*Iolani Palace contained the offices of the territorial government. In 1943 Hawaii was still a territory of the United States; it achieved statehood in 1959.

hour."

A half an hour later, my cousin was there with an Army jeep. He was a member of the motor pool at Schofield Barracks. The next thing I know, the three of us were in the jeep. I sat in the front and "Ziggie" sat in the back, and Danny was showing us the sights of Honolulu on government time and money. We bumped into quite a few of our crew members who were walking up and down the streets in Honolulu, taking in the sights. They just couldn't figure out how the hell I could be there within less than an hour and be involved in an Army jeep. They all wanted a ride. Naturally we didn't take anybody else on board, because we'd have a riot on our hands. Besides, there was no room. So we just kept on going. My cousin spent several hours giving us a tour of the island and was very happy to see me. He asked me to visit him as much as I could on every liberty.

In those days, there was a curfew that was in effect and enforced. You had to be off the streets by 10:00 o'clock at night. If you had somebody that you were staying with, you were able to have overnight liberty. I gave my address as the Schofield Barracks. I thoroughly enjoyed myself having someone who knew the island, and had wheels, rather than spending my money on taxi fares around the island.

Q: Did you go to USO or YMCA while you were there?

Mr. Bak: I spent some time in the USO when we couldn't get hold of Danny, or when he was on duty. But most of the time, he was able to take off. How he could arrange to take off when he did is beyond me. He showed me documents with a lieutenant's signature that supposedly he himself signed to get the jeep out of the base. So we did have some liberty. I remember eating at a restaurant called P. Y. Chung's. It was supposed to be the best steakhouse in Honolulu. That was a place where all the sailors that I knew of would go to have dinner. We went out for a steak, and then we'd go to the beer joints in Honolulu and mostly walk the streets looking around. The enlisted men's beer garden was a popular spot.

We just didn't seem to have too much time, because most of my time was spent with my cousin. He invited me to his girlfriend's home to meet the family. He was very serious about going with his girlfriend and eventually getting married. Her name was Barbara Silva. He introduced me to her sister, a girl by the name of Alta, a very lovely girl, about 5-7, 5-8, very attractive, a Hawaiian-Portuguese girl. So I had my dates in Honolulu with my cousin's fiancee's sister. We went out as a foursome to dinner or a nightclub somewhere in Honolulu. And, again, our shipmates couldn't understand how I could operate so fast. I guess I had a reputation of being a fast worker.

Q: You were lucky.

Mr. Bak: I was lucky, very lucky.

Q: What was it like when you were staying at the barracks? How did the other Army people receive you?

Mr. Bak: They were very nice. They made a big joke of my cousin being a corporal and I being a third class petty officer. In fact, when we went to dinner at the Army barracks, the sergeants took me with them and let my cousin eat by himself with the corporals at the regular mess. That was a big joke with them. They just dragged me with them.

Q: Was he older than you were?

Mr. Bak: Yes, he was about four years older than I was. He joined the Army, I think, around 1936, and the next thing I knew, he was stationed in Hawaii.

Q: Was the shore patrol much in evidence in Honolulu during that time?

Mr. Bak: Yes. The shore patrol was very, very much in evidence. There was always somebody patrolling, either by walking the beat, or you'd see a lot of paddy wagons and jeeps around. There just seemed to be an awful lot of sailors in town, an awful lot of Marines, an awful lot of Army people in town. Honolulu was loaded with the military.

Q: Did they keep order pretty well?

Mr. Bak: Most of what I remember, they did. Honolulu never seemed to be any kind of a problem when I was there. The thing I remember about Honolulu was the lines of sailors and soldiers and Marines waiting to go to houses of prostitution. There could have been about a hundred guys waiting in line. Some were reading newspapers, some reading magazines, and some shooting the breeze, just waiting their turn. And in the building next door there was another line of similar GIs waiting to get their prophylactic treatment in Honolulu. We never seemed to have any fights of any kind. I've never been to a bar in Honolulu or a restaurant where the sailors or the GIs were rambunctious or tearing the place apart like you would see in movies or read about.

Q: I'm surprised that the shore patrol was so tolerant of the prostitution in Hawaii, that guys could openly stand out in lines.

Mr. Bak: In the early years of the war, this was allowed. The shore patrol had no jurisdiction of the local houses of prostitution. But later on, when we came back to Honolulu, it just seemed that the lines had disappeared. Evidently, someone complained, and I guess the government put a stop to it.

Q: Did you have a chance to keep up with world affairs on board ship? Did you get news on the ship's radio?

Mr. Bak: We primarily got news from the radio shack. They published a radiogram that was available to the crew. It was a very brief listing of world events, battles, things that happened around the world.

Q: Baseball scores?

Mr. Bak: Not too many baseball scores. The only time we'd get any news like that was around World Series time. Except for the Army-Navy football game, sporting events were not a very big part of the scene at sea, because we were so busy.

Q: Did you have an idea of the strategic picture in the Pacific--of what sorts of things the Allies were doing?

Mr. Bak: No. We just, I guess, followed along with wherever the ship was going, and that was part of the thing. We had no idea what the overall strategy was. We thought we were doing very well and that we were gaining by all the advances the Navy was making during the Pacific campaigns.

Q: Which, in fact, was the case.

Mr. Bak: Which, in fact, was the case.

Q: I think the next step is to describe your experiences in battle. Why don't we save that for the next time?

Mr. Bak: Okay.

Interview Number 2 with Michael Bak, Jr.

Place: Shoney's Inn, Vienna, Virginia

Date: Tuesday, 10 April 1984

Interviewer: Paul Stillwell


Q: We talked last time about your first visit to Hawaii when you were on board the Franks in World War II. Is there anything you want to add from that period?

Mr. Bak: I think the most significant thing that happened to me when our ship pulled into Pearl Harbor was seeing the battleships sunk and the impressions we had as young sailors aboard ship who had never been in a battle zone before. We realized the war was on, and I think everybody aboard ship felt anxious to do what he could do to defeat the enemy. It was just a common bond between everybody to get the job done. I think it made a deep impression on everybody that saw that and to remember forever Pearl Harbor. It was very quiet. You steamed by with your ship, and seeing the battleship Arizona submerged in the water was just an awesome sight.

The other thing I wanted to mention was about my cousin Daniel Serafin, who was in the Army, stationed at Fort Shafter. I mentioned last time how I got together with him. Danny's girlfriend was a Hawaiian-Portuguese by the name of Barbara Silva and a very attractive young lady.

She had a sister named Alta Silva. They lived at 7557 Opela Road, Honolulu 49, Territory of Hawaii. Alta worked in the Liberty House department store in Honolulu. Eventually he married Barbara Silva, and he wanted me to go with her sister so that we could bring both of them back to the United States. I can just picture my mother, Russian-born, not knowing anything about people of foreign cultures other than the Americans and the Russians. It would have been some scene back home when the ship was coming back with Hawaiian-Portuguese wives. Anyway, I backed out of the thing.

One of the things about Danny was the fact that whenever I visited the Army barracks he had an 8 by 10 picture of his girlfriend on the table next to his cot. Every time he would dress or undress, I noticed he would always turn the picture around. I said, "Danny, why do you do that?"

He said, "Well, I don't want to have my girlfriend looking at me while I'm getting dressed and undressed so I always turn the picture around."

I'd never seen that done before or since.

Q: What were the living conditions like for the Army men there in the barracks?

Mr. Bak: Well, they were very limited. They were very meager. I remember staying overnight on a regular cot. They gave me some blankets. There were around eight soldiers in the room that I was in. I was in the cot of a soldier who was either on liberty or away from the barracks for the night.

Q: How would you compare them with the Navy barracks you had known in boot camp?

Mr. Bak: I think the Navy boot camp barracks were a little more comfortable from the standpoint of being probably more modern. They were in a location that was not as remote as an Army post, and they seemed to be much better. It just seemed like a transient type of an operation where soldiers came in and soldiers went out. But my cousin never left the island. He was stationed there for the entire war.

Q: You mentioned this feeling you had when you saw the sunken battleships there in Pearl Harbor. I know revenge had been a motive earlier. By 1943, did you still feel that way toward the Japanese?

Mr. Bak: Yes, I think everyone did. It was the common enemy. We were shocked to see it and shocked to know that somebody could do this to the Americans and get away with it. We just felt that something had to be done, and we were going to do our job, to defeat the enemy. We had to step over different islands in the South Pacific. It was going to take a little time. But it was that feeling of camaraderie, and it was just a 100% effort on everybody's part to do the job.

Q: Was there any step-up in the tempo of training and exercises and drills as you left Hawaii and went out to the war zone?

Mr. Bak: Yes, as soon as we got to Hawaii, we were in town for a short while. Then we had gunnery practice. I think we were bombarding the island of Molokai. We also had antisubmarine maneuvers. We had antiaircraft maneuvers using the 5-inch guns, quad 40s, and 20-millimeter guns. That was the first time we were operating with a larger fleet of ships than we did off San Diego. There was a training routine to get everyone familiar with the job that they were supposed to be doing while at sea.

Q: Was the pace pretty hectic during this time?

Mr. Bak: It was very hectic. We never knew when we were going to leave Hawaii. There wasn't much time to do anything other than get prepared and get your ship loaded with gear, stowing food, ammunition, and loading up with fuel. I mean, it wasn't a relaxing attitude. It was just, "Get the fellows some liberty while we're here and then get them back aboard ship because it will be months and months and months before we'll get back."

Q: Did you have any idea specifically what you would be doing, or was that covered by security?

Mr. Bak: Well, the only thing we knew was that we were going to be part of a fleet.

Q: Did you get training in the Hawaiian waters on your plane guard duties?

Mr. Bak: Yes, we had some training in Hawaiian waters, mainly with jeep carriers at that point.*

Q: I wonder how soon you knew that the Gilbert Islands would be the objective?

Mr. Bak: When we got out under way from Pearl Harbor, we had no idea whether we were going on a training mission, or whether we were going to be part of the invasion force. Because the ships took off in groups of a couple of ships here, a couple of ships there, and they would meet somewhere at a given point in the ocean and form the fleet. It wasn't just an armada of ships leaving Pearl Harbor at one time. It just seems, if I recall, we had a division of four destroyers which went together as a group, and then we

---

*The jeep carriers, known as CVEs or escort carriers, were built on merchant-type hulls. They were smaller and slower than the built-for-the-purpose attack carriers.

joined a larger group in a task force. We were assigned a task force number.

Q: Did you operate with these same destroyers time and time again in your division?

Mr. Bak: Yes. The <u>Franks</u>, the <u>Haggard</u>, the <u>Hoel</u>, and the <u>Johnston</u> were the four ships that were in our division. It was known as Destroyer Division 94.

Q: Did you have the division commodore on your ship?

Mr. Bak: I don't know why, but we never did. We only had the captain aboard ship, who was a commander.

Q: Probably just as fortunate.

Mr. Bak: Oh, yes. I enjoyed that, because it was less hectic, I would imagine, than having a flag aboard. That would cause a lot of tension probably amongst everyone to do the right thing--not that we would do anything different, but, I think, it's just the tension.

Q: Somebody else looking over your shoulder.

Mr. Bak: Yes, that's exactly right, exactly right.

Q: What do you recall of your first combat operation?

Mr. Bak: Shortly after we left Pearl Harbor, we saw the first ship sink, the Liscome Bay. Reading back in some of the books, I notice we lost 770 men on the Liscome Bay. I thought it went down in five minutes, but it went down in about 23 minutes. The book that I read said that it went down just before sunrise. It was dark out there, and I remember it was just like putting a candle out. The ball of fire was snuffed out as the ship sank.

Q: Did you get to watch the whole operation in which she was involved? How much did you see of her demise?

Mr. Bak: As soon as the carrier exploded, we went to general quarters. We watched the whole thing. We were just dumbfounded that the ship was blown up.

Q: How far away were you?

Mr. Bak: We were about 2 or 3 miles. We were in a formation. The Liscome Bay was inside the formation, and a submarine got her. We were just dumbfounded. That's the first time we experienced the horrors of war, when a ship in our own formation was hit. I think it sort of scared everybody. They just sort of felt, "My gosh, this is for real." Everybody wanted to get out to the war zone as quick as possible, myself included. "Let's get out there and, boy, we'll show them what we can do and how we're going to beat the Japs in a short time." We found out it wasn't so easy.

Q: How did the crew react? Were they any more cautious or fearful or what?

Mr. Bak: I guess they were not any more cautious, because they were cautious before that happened. They may have been more fearful. At that time, we had no idea how many men were lost, but we knew it was a lot of men lost because of the way the ship blew up and looked like a ball of fire. It just happened so fast, and there was an explosion. We knew it was a big crew. We knew there were about 1,000 men aboard that ship. We felt at least half the crew would be dead by seeing what we'd seen out there.*

Q: Did your ship have any part in rescuing survivors?

Mr. Bak: No, we didn't pick any survivors up. That was assigned to another group of destroyers that were closer to the ship. We were on the other side of the screen.

Q: What was the role of your ship in the Gilbert Islands

---

*On 23 November 1943, the escort carrier Liscome Bay (CVE-56) was torpedoed and sunk by the Japanese submarine I-175. Of her complement of some 900 officers and men, fewer than 300 were rescued.

operation?

Mr. Bak: At that time we were primarily screening the task group for submarines. We were also behind carriers to pick up pilots in a plane guard station. That's when we started to get behind the carriers and pick up pilots, if and when they crashed. These ships included the USS _Coral Sea_, USS _Corregidor_, and USS _Liscome Bay_. Our first rescue of a down plane occurred during this period. An aircraft from USS _Coral Sea_ crashed into the water during takeoff. We picked up three survivors.* Rescue was made by whaleboat. During the course of the war, the USS _Franks_ was credited with rescuing 22 pilots from the water.

A few days later, after sunset, we had our first exposure to enemy aircraft. The task force was attacked by enemy bombers. Flares were dropped all around us, making the night as bright as day. We opened fire without a hit. The bombers left without dropping a bomb. I believe that the bombers were working in conjunction with their submarines. The next night more Jap aircraft were picked up on radar but no attack was made. During the battle of Tarawa, we had patrol duty outside the lagoon entrance to protect the transports from enemy submarines. During this campaign, we picked up a pilot, Lieutenant (j.g.) Burshner, USNR, and transferred him back to the USS _Coral Sea_ via

---
*Rescued were the pilot, Clark William Marian, USNR; ARM3c James B. Bart, USN; and AOM3c A.J. Mihalik, USNR.

breeches buoy.

Q: How good were the charts of that area

Mr. Bak: The only time we had a problem was when we came to an atoll. For example, when we got down to the Gilbert Islands, our ship itself never had to go where there would be shoals or shallow water. We actually didn't go in to Tarawa itself and try to anchor. The charts were pretty good from just the invasion standpoint. However, many times the navigator would say, "That's the best we have as far as actual charts go." Because they were not up to date. Whenever we went anywhere, there was always a caution about things that might have changed.

Q: How would you describe a typical day during that operation, or elsewhere when you were in the war zone?

Mr. Bak: The watch changed every four hours. I was on duty four hours, and I was off duty eight hours. When we were off duty, the quartermaster gang and the bridge gang would usually congregate near the bridge, away from the bridge itself so that we wouldn't interrupt the flow of the activities. My day began with breakfast very early in the morning. I had the duty of winding all the clocks aboard ship, so I had the ability to roam amongst every station aboard ship that had a clock. I'd have to wind the clocks every seven days. As a result, I knew a lot of the fellows aboard ship in all the gangs aboard ship.

Q: It would be unusual for an enlisted man to have that opportunity, wouldn't it?

Mr. Bak: Very unusual, yes. I was very fortunate to be a quartermaster.

So the routine would be drills. I think in the beginning of the first invasion that we went to, we knew we were going to have enemy in the near area. It was a constant drilling by the captain and the crew to make sure they would do the job when general quarters came up. I mean, everybody bitched like hell. They would get us up in the morning. We left Pearl Harbor to go to the Gilbert islands, and I'm sure the first night out we had general quarters at least once or twice. Sometimes after that we had it three times a night just to get the guys awake and get them up to their station, and then secure after half an hour and get them back to bed again for another hour, and get them up again. We seemed to have a lot of drills at nighttime. All the gunners were at their station in the 5-inch mounts and the 40-millimeter guns and the 20 millimeters. And the torpedomen always got their torpedoes ready to fire if and when they actually had to use them, because as a screening ship they were always in a standby condition. They never knew when a submarine was going to be close by. The sonarmen were always pinging for submarines. So everybody aboard ship was doing something in preparation for any kind of action they might take, whether it was on land, or sea, or underwater.

Q: Beyond the drills you had real general quarters, too.

Mr. Bak: Well, beyond the drills we had real general quarters. The Gilbert Islands campaign was not a campaign where we saw a lot of action. It was an easy one for us at that time, because there was not much resistance from the Japanese in the Gilbert Islands. I don't think they expected us to hit there. They were expecting us to hit somewhere else, I think. As a result, the invasion itself, except at Tarawa, was pretty easy.

Q: Tarawa was very difficult.

Mr. Bak: That was very difficult, yes. From the fleet standpoint, it was very easy. We didn't see a lot of airplanes or a lot of enemy ships. There were very few, except for the Jap submarine that sank the Liscome Bay during this campaign.

Q: Was there a routine of going to GQ at dawn and dusk to protect against submarines? Many ships did have that.

Mr. Bak: Yes, we had dawn general quarters almost every morning. We always had somebody looking into the sun and keeping a sun watch. But I don't recall specifically general quarters at dusk. It's possible but not as memorable as dawn GQ, possibly because when dawn GQ would be sounded, we may have been awakened from a sound sleep, whereas at dusk we were already awake. Sunrise and sunset would be, I imagine, the best time for submarines to spot an enemy, because that's when the horizon is the clearest and the visibility is the best for silhouetting.*

Q: Was this a fatiguing routine for you, with four on, eight off, and GQs thrown in besides?

Mr. Bak: For me I think it was the toughest job because of that routine. Whenever you had general quarters, you might be going off duty, and as soon as you're off duty the general quarters alarm would sound. Or sometimes you're on general quarters for a long period of time, and then you're right in the middle of your watch, so you go right to your duty again. It was kind of fatiguing, yes. I would say from the standpoint of any rate aboard ship, it was fatiguing more so than any other rating because of the fact you're on the bridge, you're under the gun with the officers constantly: the officer of the deck, the

---
*These low visibility periods also made it difficult to spot a periscope when the submarine was approaching from the direction opposite the sun.

navigator, and the captain. I enjoyed it thoroughly, but you always had to be alert for whatever was coming up.

Q: Were the officers very strict?

Mr. Bak: No, not to me they weren't. I was very impressed with our officers. The majority of them were very good. I was always impressed by their mannerisms, their neatness, shipshape routine. They all tried to impress the captain with their ability to perform their duties. It just seemed that they were all eager to do something to help the ship, to improve the standings of the ship in the eyes of the commander of the destroyer squadron or the fleet itself. Whether we refueled at sea, whether we did anything else in a seamanship like manner, there was emphasis by all the officers to do a good job. I never had any kind of a problem with any of the officers aboard ship at all. In all my 31 months aboard the Franks, it just seemed that they were nice guys. Some were more capable than others from the standpoint of being an officer of the deck. I think that was based, a lot of it, on experience they had before coming on board.

I remember coming on board for the first time and meeting the chief quartermaster.* I felt he resented my getting a third class rate when I had never been to sea before. He told me one day it took him 12 years to become

---

*This is a reference to Chief Quartermaster Justin Grace, whom Mr. Bak also mentioned in the first interview.

a third class quartermaster in the regular Navy, and I think he sort of resented it. He never said so, but our chief quartermaster was very confident of his abilities in a very quiet sort of way. He was more of an introvert than an extrovert.

Q: Was he shy?

Mr. Bak: He was very shy. I think the shyness was caused by his feeling that he always wanted to be sure that nothing would screw up. It seemed that since regular Navy men took so long to make their ratings, they were protecting their future. Whereas sailors who were in for the duration weren't concerned about the postwar period. I guess the regular Navy guys were brought up differently than we were. I'm not knocking Chief Grace; he was very capable as a quartermaster. He knew his stuff. He helped me tremendously. He guided me. He was one of these guys who really cautioned us about chasing girls or drinking. He was always against that sort of thing. Usually sailors would pal around with each other and have cliques. He seemed to me like more of a loner, maybe because he would be in the company of chief petty officers instead of enlisted men. Sometimes when we would see him on the beach or on liberty, he'd be by himself.

Q: His behavior may have seemed unusual to you, but he was being forced to adjust to a Navy that was a lot different from the one he grew up in.

Mr. Bak: You're right. Maybe my feeling about the chief in the beginning was from my inexperience, and it probably showed. I knew very little about the chief. It just seemed that he didn't want to talk, whereas the bridge gang sat around on the flag bag or on the bridge many times just shooting the breeze. Some evenings when things were kind of quiet, you'd talk about your home, your family, your girlfriends or guys you knew at home, or whatever you did and so forth. Then, again, the chief lived in chief petty officers' mess in the forward part of the ship. We were in the after part of the ship, so we actually didn't bump into too many chiefs. The other chiefs sort of kept to themselves. All the chiefs did. I guess it was sort of a class thing. I guess they were all regular Navy guys, and they saw all the young kids come aboard. I didn't realize it then, but they were probably thinking, "Gee, look what we have aboard here. These guys have never been to sea before and have all these ratings already."

Q: Maybe these old-timers thought that you were invading their private club. When the Navy became so much bigger, they had to put up with a lot of newcomers they maybe would have preferred not to.

Mr. Bak: Yes, but after about the first year or so, when we went through a lot of different battles together, that sort of disappeared. Then we had good camaraderie. I think that once we crossed the equator and we had the initiation aboard ship, then everybody was accepted as a true sailor, I mean salty. Then we came back to Honolulu for the first time and we wore our battle ribbons on our jumpers. Then we were just like regular Navy guys. The new sailors who were coming on board for the first time, I guess, were impressed by our demeanor and so forth, like I was impressed when I saw other people.

Q: Jumping ahead a little, when you saw these new fellows, did you then have a tendency to look down on them?

Mr. Bak: We didn't look down on them, but we knew that we were saltier than they were. You felt that you had contributed to the war effort more so than being in boot camp, quartermaster school, and in training on board ship. Once you got the first taste of guns going off, then you felt a lot better about your contribution to the effort.

Q: What are your specific recollections of the shellback initiation ceremony?

Mr. Bak: One of the high points of a Navy man's career is

the day that he crosses the equator for the first time. Before you cross the equator, you are known as a "pollywog." Once you go through an initiation, you are then a salty sailor known as a "shellback." We crossed the equator for the first time on November 17th, 1943, on our way to the Gilbert Islands operation. Since we were headed for enemy waters, the initiation didn't take place until our return voyage back to Pearl Harbor. The ceremony begins with the hoisting of a jolly roger flag to the top of the mast. The officers and men who previously were initiated are in charge. All of them are dressed in various costumes depicting pirates of the raging main.

The initiation took place on the port side of the main deck and the fantail. When I was ready to be initiated, I was brought before a fearful looking chaplain who heard me confess to crimes that I was accused of, such as thinking the whaleboat is an ashtray, failing to back the attack, and being a vile and scurvy pollywog. Next, I had to crawl on my stomach under ropes that were stretched across the deck with hardly any room to maneuver. At the other end, a hose with a heavy stream of water was trained on me to wash my sins away. Meanwhile, as I am crawling on my stomach, I am being paddled on my rear end by a number of the crew who delighted in inflicting punishment. Feeling half drowned and in pain, I was ushered in front of the cameraman. When I was pushed down into a seat, I immediately jumped because it was electrically charged. They then had me stand in front of a makeshift box camera asking me to smile wide. As I did so, a stream of grease entered my mouth with joyous laughter from the crew.

At this point, I felt very sick. The ship's doctor consoled me with some pills that were guaranteed to make me feel better. Next, I was ushered in front of the ship's baby. Chief Quartermaster Grace was naked except for a diaper around his waist. I was then forced to kiss his knee that was loaded with grease. As I did so, someone held my head in that position for a few seconds. Then I met Davy Jones and Neptunus Rex and was indoctrinated as a shellback. Later on when I had to urinate, I noticed that my urine was green and I was immediately sick all over. Later I found that this the doctor's pills caused me to pee green. Everyone was initiated in this fashion. Later on when we crossed the equator again, I was able to get my revenge on the new pollywogs

Q: We talked earlier about your daily routine. What else do you recall?

Mr. Bak: Even though we were part of the fleet, it was a requirement of the Navy that every ship's navigator gave a position report for the quartermaster log every morning, at noon, and evening. As a quartermaster, I remember logging changes of direction, changes of speed. That always had to be in the log, as well as the barometer readings and temperature readings, wind velocities, and other changes that occur during the day. I remember the navigator would cross off with X's on each chart as we moved along a line from one point to the other. Day by day we would gain so many miles. Then he would check that position on the chart with his star sights. If we were steaming on a course of, say, 270, maybe for four days, we would have the line drawn that direction.

Q: Is that a rhumb line?

Mr. Bak: I guess it's called a rhumb line. Then the navigator would get his position report and run the rhumb line through.

Q: What was your role when the navigator was taking sights?

Mr. Bak: Well, first off, my role was to identify the stars. Number one, I held a timepiece with a sweep second hand that was used to mark time for the navigator. It was very important to have the exact time in minutes and seconds. Otherwise, you'd screw up the fix. When he'd give me the mark, I would take time and we would record that sighting. We'd get at least three stars in different parts of the sky. One of the nice things about the sky was the fact that each day when you travel you know the stars are going to be in a certain location. You can almost look at that point and see the first star before anybody else does. My friends thought it was impressive, but it was just a matter of the quartermaster knowing exactly the relation to where the stars were.

Q: How much familiarity was there between officers and enlisted? Did you ask them about their personal lives and so forth?

Mr. Bak: No, I never did. There was very little. They sort of kept to themselves, and we kept to ourselves. I think one of the reasons is the fact that when we wrote letters back home, they were being censored by the officers. We sort of resented the fact that they knew what we were writing. I'm sure they got a big chuckle out of reading the enlisted men's mail, and many times during the wardroom conversation, you know, bringing up certain things that were said by certain people in the letters. But there was very little camaraderie other than just the informal activities aboard ship. Perhaps it was also my feeling a bit inferior due to rank.

Q: Did the discussion with the officers stick pretty much to the job?

Mr. Bak: Yes, mostly to the job.

Q: How did you spend your spare time?

Mr. Bak: Well, I've mentioned shooting the breeze, scuttlebutt, talking about things back home. A lot of it was related to sports--what we did in high school, what sports we'd played, about baseball and different athletic events. And aboard ship there wasn't a hell of a lot more to do. A couple of guys were lifting weights. I was never a big weight lifter myself. But we had a number of guys on the fantail that used to lift weights, and I'd go back there once in a while and try my hand but nothing too much.

I also did some reading of novels that we picked up on shore or borrowed from other crew members. Most of my reading time was spent on studying my quartermaster manuals, preparing for advancement. The only book I kept with me aboard ship was More Power to Your Words by Clement Wood.

Q: Did you spend much time on flashing light and semaphore and so forth?

Mr. Bak: I was just looking at some of the pictures of the USS Franks crew that I got since I saw you last. In one of the pictures is a fellow by the name of John Barbee, who was a second class signalman. He was a little bit ticked off at me in the beginning because of an incident when a message was coming across. I was able to read it, and I gave it to Captain Lidstone.* I happened to be right alongside the captain. Barbee then came by and gave the same message to the captain. The captain said to him, "Oh, yes. Bak just gave me that message." So I made no friends. I think for a while the signalmen resented my intrusion of their domain. But after that, we got over the whole thing, because many times I was able to stand watch for them and give them a hand when they wanted to take a break or go to the bathroom.

Q: So it was not typical for a quartermaster to be able to do signalman duties?

Mr. Bak: No, not really, but you were required to know some signalling to get your rate. I'm only judging by myself. You were supposed to know it, but I don't recall any of our quartermasters, including the chief, able to read light or send semaphore as well as signalmen. But I thoroughly enjoyed it.

Q: How was the pay during wartime?

Mr. Bak: As a first class quartermaster, I think, I was making about $150 a month. I think we started off at about $75 a month in boot camp.

---
*Commander Nicholas A. Lidstone, USN, was the first commanding officer of the Franks.

Q: I would have guessed lower than that.

Mr. Bak: Maybe, $50 a day once a month. There was a song about that, $50 a day once a month. It might have been less than that.

Q: When you were in the war zone, was there a tendency for the men to just leave their money on the books rather than drawing it?

Mr. Bak: The only time we drew money out was when we went to a liberty port. Once we left Honolulu, there was nothing out there to buy anyway. I can't recall any of those islands where you could spend any money. So everybody left their money on the books. A lot of fellows just sent a certain amount of money home. It automatically went through payroll deductions. I think we had some small stores where we bought cigarettes, toiletries, and things like that.

Q: Shaving cream?

Mr. Bak: Shaving cream, razor blades. Yes, we always bought those. Whatever the ship's store had. It was only open at a certain time of day. I can't recall exactly when, but that was another part of the routine, going to the ship's store and buying some stuff.

Q: Did someone in each division take up all the laundry for the division, or did you have to do it individually?

Mr. Bak: I don't recall. It just seems to me that each guy brought his laundry bag down to the laundry shop whenever he wanted to. We'd usually get a pillow case, stuff our dirty laundry in a pillow case, and bring it down there. Everything was stamped and you'd get it back.

Q: You were talking about Chief Grace. Even though he was withdrawn and quiet, he brought you along so you could run the quartermaster gang. So he must have been pretty skilled at imparting his knowledge.

Mr. Bak: Well, he was very skilled. I think one of the things I should mention was that he used to take the wheel whenever we had fueling operations. With Captain Lidstone, Chief Grace was the only one who was on the wheel going alongside a tanker, a carrier, cruiser, or battleship to refuel. I admired the guy keeping 60 feet between the carrier or tanker and our ship and preventing the fuel hoses from parting. I remember once when Captain Stephan was in command, we had a problem when we were alongside the battleship New Jersey.* I believe one of the fuel hoses broke. Captain Stephan was very upset. The swells were very bad. From that point on, he wouldn't let the chief take the wheel anymore. He yelled for me, "Bak, take the wheel." Fortunately, I was able to hold the ship steady without incident. That was my indoctrination. So it was a kind of a salty thing, a great experience, a neat thing keeping that ship 60 feet away and keep spinning the wheel back and forth, bringing the fantail in, bringing the bow in and the fantail out. I, fortunately, never had a parting of the hoses. Chief Grace was transferred from the Franks shortly after that, so I was the senior quartermaster for the rest of my time on board.

Q: What kind of orders would you get? Would you get a course to steer, half a degree to change?

Mr. Bak: Well, each ship was on a certain course. From that point on, you were on your own. For example, if the other ship was on 090, our course had to be 090. It was just a touch of turning the wheel slightly one way and then slightly the other way. You could never have the ship itself sitting there permanently. You had to sort of ease the wheel around constantly to keep that rudder in a position that it would move the ship in the direction that you wanted to go.

---

*Commander David R. Stephan, USN, commanding officer from 30 June 1944 to 2 April 1945.

Q: Would you do this by seaman's eye, watching the bigger ship?

Mr. Bak: By seaman's eye and by feel. But mainly by seaman's eye--watching the other ship and the swells, and watching the bow of the <u>Franks</u> and the fuel ship. That was the key. If we were alongside the carrier and it wasn't too windy, that wasn't too bad, because you had the protection on the leeward size of the otehr ship for an easier ride. If, on the other hand, the wind direction changed, then you had a problem. You couldn't shift direction with another ship once the fueling started.

Q: Now, how much would you have to do that yourself, and how much depended on orders from the skipper?

Mr. Bak: He would guide you alongside the refueling ship with course directions. However, once all lines and hoses were in place, you were mostly on your own. He'd be watching the ships' distance as well as you were. He was always out there on the side of the bridge, looking down. So he always knew exactly where the ship was. He would leave me alone. Sometimes he would yell out if the ship wasn't in the proper position. You have to be alert at all times to keep the ship on course. It was kind of a relief when it was all done. Seamanship, I think, was a criterion for judging captains in their performance of their duties for future ranks. If the ship didn't screw up, they got good marks and good reports. But if the ship screwed up because of some crew member, it was still the captain's fault. He was in charge, so that's why I think the captain was always concerned about making sure we did a good job.

Q: Was Chief Grace resentful after you took over that job?

Mr. Bak: He wasn't really resentful towards me. I don't think he liked the captain. He was just resentful of the captain. Captain Lidstone trusted Chief Grace with every aspect of the chief's duty. Captain Stephan, on the other hand, was a difficult person to deal with.

Q: How did he get along with Lidstone?

Mr. Bak: Lidstone never gave him a bad time. Lidstone liked the chief. He respected the chief for his many years of service in the Navy. I think he was glad to have him aboard, because his was a brand-new ship. Grace was the only quartermaster who had been at sea before.

Q: What do you remember about Captain Lidstone as an officer, a leader, a personality aboard ship?

Mr. Bak: As an officer, well qualified and well trained.

As a leader, he was well respected by the officers and crew. Where Lidstone was a very capable officer, he was also reserved, quiet, never raised his voice, never seemed to make a snap decision, just a good seaman.

Q: Did the crew like him?

Mr. Bak: They liked him. They respected him. I don't think he was the kind of a guy to get warm to. I don't think if I saw him down the street in Honolulu, I'd want to be in his company.

Q: Why not?

Mr. Bak: Well, probably knowing that he was a naval officer from the Annapolis Naval Academy and probably had a hell of a lot more experience in the world than I did, and probably frowned on some of the things we did as young boys: drinking beer or visiting the different parts of the liberty ports.

Q: So it wasn't Lidstone per se, though; it was people of his rank and position.

Mr. Bak: Yes. It was a rank that we were in awe of. Hell, I never saw a naval officer until I got to boot camp. The only time I ever saw a Navy ship was in the 1930s when we saw an article in the paper one day, "The Fleet's In, Destroyers in the Hudson River." Somebody had a car, and he drove us over to the bluffs of New Jersey Palisades, and down below were some destroyers and ships in the river.

Q: Could you describe the process by which Chief Grace brought you along and trained you and made you steadily more capable? How good was he as a teacher?

Mr. Bak: With the chief, it just seems to me that he must have joined the Navy many years ago as a young boy and been out at sea all his life, just struggling along to get to where he was as a chief quartermaster. But he brought me along very nicely. He showed me the duties and where and what to expect, what the station was. Usually he gave you a rundown on the captain--how to behave aboard ship, what the captain's looking for. It was important that our station give 100% effort. He wanted to make sure that his quartermaster gang was in tip-top shape. He gave us a rundown of all the charts, took care of all the compasses, cleaned them up, and made sure the binoculars were handy. We were responsible, all of us, for the gear. Keeping the bridge clean, and basically just watching over. I remember him constantly watching our entries in the log, making sure that we entered all the things that happened aboard ship. So Chief Grace was helpful in that way, just by guiding people who had never been at sea before. He was also very helpful in preparing you for the next rate. He was a good source of information regarding taking tests for advancement.

Q: How much emphasis or interaction did you have with boatswain's mates of the watch since you were all up there at the same time?

Mr. Bak: Whenever we made preparations to get under way, refueled the ship at sea, took on supplies from another ship, rescued pilots, returned pilots, or were docking or coming into an anchorage, we always had a boatswain's mate on the bridge with a set of earphones. He acted as the communications link between the captain and the boatswain's mates below who were involved in one of the activities mentioned. The boatswain's gang were tough, able-bodied seamen. There was, however, a class distinction between the quartermasters and the boatswain's mates. We always pictured them as deck apes who handled all the tough assignments aboard ship. I don't remember, however, calling them deck apes to their face for fear of reprisal.

Q: So there was a kind of snobbishness among the quartermasters.

Mr. Bak: There was a kind of snobbishness among the

quartermasters. But the ship was so small you couldn't be too snobbish, because after the first couple of months at sea it just seemed like everybody meshed together pretty nicely.

Q: What was life like in your living compartment? How much room did you have?

Mr. Bak: Well, the first part of my time aboard ship, there was very little room. We had a bunk that was three-tiered, that whenever you got up in the morning and you fixed your bunk, you had to lash or chain your bunk flat against the bulkhead. They remained that way until a certain time in the evening when you could go back to your bunk and lie down. I don't think you had more than a foot and a half, 2 feet between your bunk and the one above you. Below the lower bunk was a foot locker that was very small, approximately 24 inches by 24 inches by 12 inches high. The compartment was very crowded, not much room at all. Then, later on, I was transferred to another compartment with about 12 crew members. We were all radarmen, signalmen, sonarmen, or quartermasters. We were all in the same area. Usually if you had a higher rate, you had a little better bunk. But it was very crowded. Whenever you had to sit down to go to the bathroom, you would just sit alongside five other guys, either reading a newspaper or magazine, and do your duty. Showers were open. The showers were very small and limited in space.

Q: What about the supply of fresh water? Wasn't that also limited?

Mr. Bak: That was also limited. We had to be very careful with the water, because there wasn't much water at all. It depended where we were. If we were out to sea for quite some time, then we had a problem. If we were pretty close to land, why, they'd let us use the fresh water. Most of the time we did have enough fresh water to take showers. But you never stood in the shower too long.

Q: Where did you write your letters? They didn't have tables in these compartments, did they?

Mr. Bak: No, they didn't have tables. It was a combination of many places. If the day was nice and the weather was real nice, we'd sit on the deck, the main deck or on the bridge or in the charthouse. I did most of my letter writing in the radio shack, because I was a typist and it was faster for me to type a letter than it was to write by hand. In fact, last week I found a letter I typed. I remember writing the letter many years ago to my family, telling them to tell my girlfriend not to wait for me. It was a "Dear Barbara letter" instead of a "Dear John letter." I wrote my family to tell her. I don't know why

I didn't have the balls to write her myself, but I didn't. And I've still got that letter. I was just kind of disappointed the way I wrote it. I said I didn't want to be tied down. "I don't know when I'm coming back. I'm going to be very busy and I don't want anyone waiting for me. I don't know what's going to happen out there."

Q: How did she take it? Did you ever hear?

Mr. Bak: I never heard from her after that. A very lovely girl, very pretty. I'm sure she made some fellow a very, very wonderful wife. At that time, I just felt it was a neat thing going to the South Pacific in destroyer duty. I just was looking forward to it.

Q: But it wasn't something that you wanted to share with her.

Mr. Bak: No, no, nothing to share with her at all. I did share with my family all my different things that occurred, and another friend of mine. But as far as to a girl, I got letters from different girls that I knew. But it was never the kind of letter, a waiting for you or that type of a thing at all. I didn't believe in that.

Q: How was the food on board ship?

Mr. Bak: The food was, at times, very good--at times, terrible. It was good if we were in an area where we had access to a supply ship, a destroyer tender. In the South Pacific, in the area of Bougainville, Treasury Islands, that part of the world, Espiritu Santo, we were getting Australian mutton. I remember one time when we tasted it, and it was very bad. The food was, I would say, bad in the farthest areas away from the battle zone, because there wasn't much out there. You couldn't hold much food aboard ship. We had to rely on other ships supplying our ship with the food. I know we always had some refrigeration breakdowns when we had mutton coming aboard ship. There was always an entry in the log, refrigeration broke down so they could get other foods from other ships. I think it was deliberate, you know, to throw the food overboard. But the food, to me, was not too bad because coming from the background of our family living, food was always very scarce. To me it was plentiful. I enjoyed the beans on Wednesdays and Saturday mornings and red lead we called it.

Q: What's red lead?

Mr. Bak: Catsup. I enjoyed that. But then you had powdered eggs in the morning with sandwiches. I loved Spam, an awful lot of Spam, and occasional meats you had, chicken and whatnot. It always seemed that the first meal coming back to a tender we always had a king-size meal. It was always with the goodies and the ice cream and everything else. But after that, once you got under way for four or five days, we were bitching like hell; the food was lousy.

Q: Did you have an ice cream machine on board?

Mr. Bak: No. We never had an ice cream machine at all. I was reading in the battleship navy, these guys would go down to the geedunk stand and buy ice cream. My God, they were living in luxury! Having chocolate sodas; I couldn't believe that. I never was on a battleship, so I didn't know what the duty was like aboard ship. But they had that facility. They also had movies, which we never did while we were under way. The only time we ever got ice cream was from the aircraft carriers whenever we picked up a pilot. They would give you a drum of ice cream as a reward for returning their pilot safely. But that was a rare thing.

Q: That gave you some incentive to get these guys out of the water, didn't it?

Mr. Bak: That gave us a great incentive, yes. That was a good incentive. But I think we did it even without the incentive of the ice cream. I think the attitude was, "One of our guys is down; let's help the guy." Everybody really just busted his jump. The poor bastard sometimes would come aboard after being rescued with his face all bloodied up, just a mess. It was a duty to perform, and we performed it well. We felt good about it if we rescued the pilot. And many times you wouldn't find the pilot if it was at nighttime. Sometimes during the daytime a plane went down so fast it never came up and you couldn't even find a body around or anything like that. Or sometimes the poor guy half drowned before somebody got to him.

Q: I wonder if the swimmer's harness was Navy-wide or whether the Franks developed it?

Mr. Bak: I believe that it was developed on board the Franks. Three swimmers used the harness during rescue operations. Physically, they often said the harness was tough on their midsection. On February sixth, 1945, Captain Stephan held a meritorious mast, presenting the Bronze Star Medal to Arnold Hector Baddis, SF1c, USNR; Franklin Allen Calloway, S1c, V6, USNR; and Melvin Jett Collins, Rdm3c, V-6S, USNR, for meritorious performance as swimmers, assisting in the rescue of aviation personnel in distress at sea, during the Leyte campaign.

Q: Did your ship go back into base after the Gilberts operation finished up?

Mr. Bak: We came back to Pearl Harbor for one week to

refuel, take on supplies, and get more ammunition. I should point out that whenever we were under way, going to or returning from a mission, we always conducted gunnery exercises. Each ship in the formation had plenty of opportunities to shoot their guns. At the same time, friendly aircraft would be simulating dive-bomber and strafing attacks on the fleet.

Q: Was that a warm-up operation for you in a sense, to get you ready for the rest of the war?

Mr. Bak: It was a warm-up exercise for the Navy. It was our first offensive, and we had an easy time of it. As a result of this campaign, the Navy, Marines, and Army perfected their method of amphibious warfare which proved helpful in future island-hopping campaigns.

We came back to Pearl Harbor for two weeks of upkeep and repairs. We spent five days in dry dock with all hands chipping paint. Then we went out again with five aircraft carriers and nine destroyers and returned a few days later. About a month later, the Kwajalein campaign started.* We had a little more activity with the enemy in the Marshalls than we'd had in the Gilberts, because the Japanese were preparing for us now. They could almost guess where the next stop was going to be. So we had more activity with

---

*On 31 January 1944, the Marine Corps hit the beaches in the invasion of Kwajalein Atoll, the principal target in the Marshal Islands.

bogey aircraft.

Q: What was it like to be in an air attack?

Mr. Bak: It was nice to be on a destroyer if you were in a fleet, because the Japanese always went after the biggest ships first. Usually the dive-bombers would go after the aircraft carriers or battleships, drop their bombs, and take off. Rarely did they go after the destroyer. The only time that they came deliberately at us was when somebody was being shot down or damaged and couldn't climb anymore. They would try to crash into us. So we had airplanes coming down from all angles. The problem we had sometimes, I think, was trying to keep from shooting your own ships while aiming at the planes.

We were helpless to do anything. We were sort of like a spectator. We had no guns that we were involved in as quartermasters or signalmen on the bridge. I remember specifically one time a Jap plane dropped a bomb right in the middle of the Yorktown, right smack in the middle of it.* As he was coming up, he came over about 50 yards or 100 yards from our ship and gave us his hand to his nose. I could see it very clearly. We shot him down, so it was a very busy day. I think the biggest air attacks that I witnessed were two we had between the Philippine Islands and Formosa. One going out to the South China Sea with the

---
*This incident took place on 18 March 1945, when the Franks was operating as part of Task Group 58.4.

fast carrier forces to attack China. Then on the way back, when they had all those hundreds and hundreds of Japanese planes up there. They were coming in from all angles. They would always go after our big ships. If we were in formation, they might go after a straggler or two of the destroyers. The only time the destroyers really got hit very badly was if we were 60-80 miles in front of the whole group as a picket ship, trying to find these radar pips coming in, enemy bogeys, and then we'd report them to the fleet. That's when you would get the biggest brunt of the attack, when you're by yourself and the planes are coming at you that way. But usually if we were in a formation, we always stuck to a formation and we would just shoot at the first plane coming at us. But they usually went after the big guys.

Q: Did you feel any frustration that you personally didn't get to fire a gun at them?

Mr. Bak: Well, no, I just thought I was a spectator while performing my duties. It was a hell of a ball game, you know, just watching what's going on.

Q: Well, this is a different kind of a ball game. This is one where the spectators can get killed.

Mr. Bak: Well, that's true, too. But we had, I thought, pretty good gunners. Looking back I found records our ship was credited with shooting down six planes during our time. I'm sure we had a couple that we hit that we didn't get credit for, that somebody else finished off, because there is so much shooting going on. The sky was just full of black pockmarks. It looked like black clouds all over the sky, thousands of them. We would shoot and fire these 5-inch guns sometimes, and when the enemy planes came in close, we would fire our quad 40s. There were marks all over the sky. It was amazing to see how it would look with all these ships around firing and planes going, our planes and theirs. It was a little bit like a movie sometimes that you were watching from the balcony of a theater, because there was a lot of activity going on, all over. You didn't know where to look. During this time, I had to log the things that were happening to the Franks.

Q: Did you feel a sense of excitement when this was happening?

Mr. Bak: Oh, I did, yes, very much so, very much so. You could look over the starboard side and see something that was going on, or the port side. A ship coming over here, another plane was shooting. All the gunners were ready and willing to shoot, because they wanted to get credit for an airplane to be knocked down. And they were kind of, I guess, like scoring baskets in a basketball game. They wanted to get a score.

Q: I think there's a self-preservation instinct that takes over, too, when a plane is coming right at you.

Mr. Bak: Oh, yes. That's for sure. One time, I must mention, I saw an airplane dead ahead, coming at us right above the horizon. According to my records we were about 90 miles from Kyushu on 18 March 1945, part of Task Group 58.4, which was launching planes as scheduled. The <u>Yorktown</u> was hit by a bomb from a Jap bomber, killing five and wounding 26. The <u>Intrepid</u> was struck by a bomb from a Jap Betty, killing two and wounding 43. We had two quad 40s, one on the port side and one on the starboard. Tom Wild was captain of one of the gun crews.* I was looking ahead and I saw this plane coming in low, right for the bridge. I thought we'd had it. Tom Wild's gun crew kept shooting. You could see the tracers go right into the plane. Then the plane exploded, and it crashed into the water. That was very impressive. That was the closest that I'd seen us come to getting hit.

We had a lot of busy times with airplanes. Between Formosa and the Philippine Islands was the greatest amount of air traffic that I'd seen with planes. We had 200, 300, 400 Japanese planes, at least 200 planes coming down. You

---
*Gunner's Mate Second Class Thomas A. Wild, Jr.

could hear the TBS--enemy aircraft, 200 strong and being intercepted by our people, a lot of them getting through, the standby to fire and general quarters--that whole routine.* We had a very good method of warning the fleet when the bogeys were coming in. It just seemed that we always had either the picket ships, or airplanes of our fleet that were reporting. We knew exactly what angle they were coming in on. Every once in a while we were surprised.

The biggest surprise we had was the battle off Samar at Leyte Gulf when the Japanese fleet was just about 18 miles away without anybody knowing about it.** That's what surprised the hell out of us. I could look over the horizon and see those masts sticking up on the horizon like toothpicks. I couldn't believe it. That was the time when the three ships went in for a torpedo run. The Johnston finally got blown out of the water; she was part of our squadron. But that was not an airplane battle. That was a battle of ships; that was a surface action.

Q: Were there any carriers that you particularly enjoyed working with?

Mr. Bak: We worked with them all, with every carrier out there, I think. The Yorktown, I enjoyed that and I

---
*TBS stood for "talk between ships"--the voice radio network.
**This surface gun battle took place on 25 October 1944.

remember very well the Hancock, the Intrepid, the Belleau Wood. Small carriers--the St. Lo, Coral Sea, Liscome Bay, the Gambier Bay. We had four carriers in our division. I think Task Force 38.1 was the biggest one we were in. It was the Yorktown, the Wasp, and then the Cowpens and the Monterey. There were four carriers that we were operating with primarily during that part of the war, those four carriers. Those were the carriers that were involved with at the same time we were in the typhoon in December 1944.

Q: How well did your ship ride?

Mr. Bak: I thought it rode very well in calm, smooth waters. In a storm it was a bumpy, rolling, and pitching ride. I think the biggest problem was that it took a long time to make a turn with only one rudder to guide you in the water. So from that standpoint it took a bigger arc to make a circle. Looking back right now, I can remember that the bigger ships must have had an easier ride. But looking at our ship, My God, we were frequently pitching and rolling. But that was an accepted norm with destroyer sailors. We just didn't know any better, so we accepted it.

Q: You were all in the same boat.

Mr. Bak: We were all in the same boat.

Q: If people had a seasickness problem, did they tend to get weeded out of the crew?

Mr. Bak: We had seasickness problems only in the beginning of our entry into the Pacific Ocean. I think after the first two weeks, the seasickness problem disappeared. Once or twice, we had somebody leave our ship because they were so sick they couldn't get over it.

Q: After the Marshall Islands operation, I see by the ship's history that you escorted the transport Clay and went to the Ellice Islands. Do you recall that and moving into the Third Fleet operations?

Mr. Bak: Yes. We escorted the USS Clay to Guadalcanal in the Solomons. Along the way, we made a possible sub contact and dropped two patterns of 11 depth charges each. No positive evidence of a sinking. Also on the same date, March 13, 1944, we crossed the international date line. The date changed from March 13 to March 15, 1944. My birthdate was March 14. As a result, I never had a 21st birthday. It was also the time we teamed up with ships from Destroyer Squadron 47--the McCord, Hailey, Hoel, Heermann, and Hazelwood.

Q: Did this put a different requirement on you as a

quartermaster when you're in antisubmarine work, as opposed to steaming with the carriers?

Mr. Bak: No, from a quartermaster standpoint it was just the same. I had no other duty during watch hours and general quarters than to be on the bridge as the assistant to the navigator and the officer of the deck. For example, I never had the earphones at all. Usually a radarman or a radioman came up on the bridge to man the phones. The biggest assignment I had was to make sure the battle lights were changed on the panels. We had a panel of green, red, and white lights. Three up top of the mast, three in the middle of the mast, and three down below. They had to be changed every six hours, according to the code that was set up by the fleet commander. I always changed those things. My main job, I would say, during all this activity would be to log everything as it was happening.

Q: How much formality was there in uniforms? Did you generally wear dungarees during these actions?

Mr. Bak: Yes. During the actions we always had dungarees on. As a matter of fact, we had a strict rule about having your sleeves rolled down and full dungarees on, even though it was very hot. I guess if we had a problem with burns, it would be helpful to have cloth over the skin. I very seldom ever saw fellows in a war zone walking around with their sleeves rolled up like you might see a real tough, macho guy.

Q: How much damage control training did you get?

Mr. Bak: I didn't get any training in damage control at all. We had damage control people on the bridge in a standing-by position. Somebody was assigned to that area for damage control, like they were assigned to every other part of the ship, but I myself was not. I don't recall a duty that I had to perform during damage control, except to assist the repair party if necessary.

Q: How strict was the discipline on board the Franks?

Mr. Bak: I think the discipline was very good. I think the crew respected the officers aboard the ship. It was a very easy type of discipline because everyone seemed to be enjoying their job. It wasn't a tough duty kind of a thing, other than the general quarters and constant training. The discipline was very strong as far as the watches were concerned. Other than combat and watch situations, the discipline was very relaxed. There was always a great desire for the officer of the deck to make sure everyone was on watch looking out the way they were supposed to be. If you weren't performing your duties, somebody would get on your fanny and really jump down your throat. But I think most of the guys were trying to do their job, and as a result would accept any kind of discipline. None of the fellows seemed to mind too much. They resented probably Captain Stephan. In their minds he was a very tough guy.

Q: Were there many captain's masts?

Mr. Bak: I don't recall logging any captain's masts aboard our ship, except this one officer that we had a problem with, Ensign Thorson.*

Q: What was the problem with him?

Mr. Bak: I just think that he went psycho. I think that he didn't want to be in the war zone. I don't think he liked being on a destroyer. I don't think he liked to participate in what we were doing. And he did everything just the opposite. I think he purposely, deliberately acted like he did to get off that ship. That's my own feeling. Ensign Thorson was a likable guy. He was healthy looking, blond, handsome guy. But he was a rascal. That's what he was. He locked himself in his room and would get on the microphone that would be connected with all the speakers aboard ship. He would say, "This is 'Big T'." Like a disc jockey giving us a blow by blow of how terrible

―――――
*Ensign R.J. Thorson, USNR, who reported to the Franks in August 1944.

the ship was, how terrible the officers are aboard ship, saying things like, "While you bastards are out there eating the crap, the food in the wardroom is much better." He was really knocking the officers aboard ship very badly. But I think it acted in a reverse psychology with the crew. We enjoyed it more from a humor standpoint than taking his side that we were being screwed for some reason by the officers. But that's a situation that got out of hand. I remember eventually we transferred him to either a destroyer tender or one of the transports anchored in the harbor. We transferred him off the ship. I don't know what happened to him after that.

Q: Well, I would guess he wouldn't last very long on board with that kind of behavior.

Mr. Bak: He wanted to get out, and he got out. He just didn't like it, didn't want to do anything. He was the only guy I ever saw aboard ship that really was antisocial.

Q: Did you see or remember any cases on the one hand of a particular bravery, or on the other hand of cowardice?

Mr. Bak: Well, bravery we witnessed constantly when the fellows swam to rescue pilots downed in the water. You never knew if sharks were around. And when one of the pilots was bleeding as a result of injuries, I would imagine that would attract sharks. Bravery? I don't think there was any individual brave thing that happened, other than the fellows that swam, rescuing pilots. I would say they were the bravest guys we had. I should also give credit to the gun captains who, with their crews, manned their guns with confidence and dedication during battle. Then, too, I shouldn't forget the men in the engine rooms who never saw what was going and who were sort of trapped below. I was glad to be above decks.

Q: Did you see any cases of cowardice?

Mr. Bak: No, I didn't see any cases of cowardice at all. Again, I was limited to the bridge. And looking back, I felt kind of bad because I never knew what was going on on the fantail on board our destroyer while I was on the bridge constantly. I could see back there, but I was never there physically with the gang on the fantail, whatever they were doing. There might have been cowardice, but I don't know of any cowardice aboard ship at all.

Q: I would think the word would have spread had there been.

Mr. Bak: It would have spread, yes. Like it spread for

the officer who jumped overboard, Lieutenant Crabbe.*

Q: What was the role of the petty officers in running the ship? You say there were not captain's masts. I would think then that problems were handled at a lower level to keep them from getting up to the captain.

Mr. Bak: I don't know whether it was that way with all destroyers, but we seemed to be a group that got along fairly well.

Q: Was there any disrespect toward petty officers?

Mr. Bak: After a while, the petty officer rank didn't mean anything on a destroyer, other than a chief or first class petty officer who ran their specific assignments without fanfare. Once you got at sea, you had your dungarees on. Nobody had a petty officer badge on. You were a petty officer in name only, from the standpoint that you had the rating. They knew that you had a rating. The chief petty officers always wore their chiefs' caps. When you were at sea, nobody gave a crap. When you were on land, you were on liberty and you put your badge on that you were a petty officer; then everybody knows you're a petty officer. But on a destroyer it wasn't as class-conscious as they had on a battleship, for example. I never felt that it really was

---
*This incident, involving Lieutenant C.R. Crabbe, USNR, is discussed in greater detail later in the oral history.

hot stuff that I was a third class petty officer, or a second class petty officer, really hot stuff, or as a first class petty officer. I just felt I was one of the gang, doing the job I was supposed to be doing as part of the whole thing. Perhaps some of the regular Navy sailors felt differently. I was in the reserve Navy, doing my duty for the duration.

Q: I think part of that, too, is the fact that when you're on the bridge, you're in a rotation watch. So you didn't have too much contact with your counterparts.

Mr. Bak: We had no contact at all. We had four and eight. We only had three guys in the quartermaster gang; that's all we had. You couldn't be chickenshit, because there were only three of us to do the duty. You're in charge of a three-man operation. I would imagine with some of the other gangs aboard ship that were much larger that there was more concern about seniority. For example, the signal gang was much larger than the quartermaster gang. We probably had about eight or nine signalmen aboard ship, whereas we had only three quartermasters. So they may have had a class status there. I remember the first class signalman we had, a fellow by the name of Pappy Wood. He was really in charge of the signal gang. And John Barbee was the second class signalman; he was the second in command. He was a classic example of a regular Navy petty officer. He had been in the Navy for about six or seven years, so it showed there. But the fellows who came in after the war started, I don't believe they ever got to the class status. The captain announced that you made your rating, and that was it. No ceremonies.

Q: Did you have to take an exam?

Mr. Bak: We had a specific exam for each rate.

Q: Did you have rate training books to study?

Mr. Bak: We had a quartermaster book for each rate that listed the requirements. For example, the second class quartermaster training course had seven specific assignments that had to be successfully completed. One assignment was signalling, which I loved. We had to be able to transmit and receive five-character code groups by flashing light at the rate of eight groups per minute and a plain language message by semaphore at the rate of 100 characters per minute. Looking back, the actual on-the-job training and the helpful assistance of the navigator and Chief Grace made advancement that much easier.

Q: Why were there so many more signalmen than quartermasters?

Mr. Bak: You needed at least three men on signal watch at one time, one on each side of the bridge and one in charge of the watch. You had three watch sections, hence the larger gang.

Q: Were there any other events specifically that you remember from the spring of 1944, before you moved into the Marianas campaign?

Mr. Bak: We hit an island called Mussau one time. Our ship was designated to blow up either a fuel dump or radio tower on a small island. It stuck in my mind because it was an odd name, Mussau Island. I remember receiving a native chief and some Australian aboard our ship. We steamed by ourself all during the night. We left the formation. We got there just before sunrise. It was still dark. I was on the bridge, and this native chief pointed out a location by finger to our gunnery officer the place where a gasoline dump or radio tower was located. When we had that bearing down, we bombarded. We threw a lot of 5-inch shells into the target. Then we saw an explosion and a large fire. As soon as we saw the explosion and fire, we took off and beat it out of there, because we didn't know how many Japs were on the island. We had no idea what gun emplacements there were. I think we caught them by surprise. And we blew up the target before they knew what was going on. It was a hit and run, very successful.*

Q: Where did you get the native chief?

Mr. Bak: I don't know where he came from. He came aboard from one of our other ships. A captain's gig came by with an Australian officer and the native chief. He was with us for about two or three days, and then we put him back on another ship.

Q: And you also spent some time down in the Solomons. Do you recall that?

Mr. Bak: We spent a lot of time in the Solomons. One of our assignments was patrolling as a screen for minelayers laying mines in the Buka Passage. In fact, we sank a submarine off the island of Buka in the Solomons. A submarine was spotted in the area.** As a result, they dispatched a destroyer division to hunt for the sub. I think three or four of us cans went out to look for the sub.*** With the combination of all of us, we were able to sink a submarine. I do remember when we threw the depth

---

*The official history of the USS Franks indicates that this operation took place on 23 March 1944.
**This action, on 16 May 1944, resulted in the sinking of the Japanese submarine I-176. Also involved in the attack besides the Franks were the destroyers Haggard and Johnston.
***Destroyer Division 94 comprised the Franks (DD-554), Haggard (DD-555), Hailey (DD-556), and Johnston (DD-557)--four consecutive hull numbers.

charges over, that we thought we got the sub, because there was a tremendous mushroom type of upheaval directly astern of our ship, and we saw a lot of debris in the water. We picked a lot of junk out of the water. A whaleboat with Ensign Snell in charge was dispatched to retrieve the floating debris.* At our last ship's reunion in October of 1987, in San Antonio, Texas, we were reminiscing about the sub we sank.** Lieutenant (j.g.) Sigurd E. Swenson, our supply officer at the time of the sinking--he is currently an attorney in San Antonio--said that Ensign Snell's crew also picked up some condoms out of the water, along with the rest of the floating remains.

We spent time in the area of Bougainville in the Solomon Islands and around the Treasury islands. We saw a lot of PT boats. We never operated with PT boats, but we often observed them coming in and out of the Treasury Islands. That was one of their bases. We did a lot of screening at that time for different ships, including minelayers in that area itself. At one time we had a duty of screening a bunch of LSTs, ten knots. It was one of the worst duties we ever had, going very slow, because those ships were very slow. But that wasn't for a long time. That was a couple of days, and that was it.

Q: Did you ever feel any compassion for the guys who were

---
*Ensign W.A. Snell, USNR.
**The reunion was held following the interview, so this particular section was inserted by Mr. Bak in the course of his subsequent work on the transcript.

in the submarine on the other side?

Mr. Bak: No, none whatsoever. It was us or them. We thought they were a bunch of bastards. The faster we killed them off, the faster the war would be over. Because of what they did to Pearl Harbor and all those guys who died there, nobody had any compassion for the Japanese. I mean, it was just a universal, all-out effort to beat the Japs. I would have hated to be on the Japanese side.

Q: Did you hate them?

Mr. Bak: Yes, I did. I just wanted to get rid of them and get back to civilian life. I, myself, was never a regular Navy guy. I was in the Navy because of the war, and I thought I would do my part by participating and helping destroy the enemy.

Q: Your ship bombarded Shortland Island on 20 May. Do you remember that?

Mr. Bak: Only that we were fired upon by enemy shore where we bombarded when the Marines went in, or the GIs that went in. Our job was to bombard the islands in a certain designated area, based on a chart. I remember we had those grid charts with lettering on it, A7 or A5, or whatever the case may be. The Marines had the enemy spotted somewhere, we would lob over shells at a certain spot. They would give us a radio contact, "Up 50, down 50, on target, right 50, left 50," whatever the case may be, just to support the landings. We did an awful lot of bombarding of islands that way. Every once in a while shells would come off the beach shooting at us. And, fortunately, we never were hit. We did a lot of that bombarding.

Q: Did CIC run the show in your ship on the bombardment?*

Mr. Bak: Yes. They always ran the show. They were the ones who set up the targets, and they gave the gunnery officer the range and what direction to shoot at.

Q: They have to know very precisely the ship's position so they can calculate the angle in relation to the target.

Mr. Bak: Yes, because you're not standing still. You're constantly moving. There again, that's where the PPI scope of the radar came in handy to show where you were in relation to the targets.

Q: After that, you went to the Marianas campaign. How much was the Franks involved in that?

---

*CIC--combat information center.

Mr. Bak: We were in everything. We bombarded Saipan, Tinian, and Rota, the three islands. In fact, if I recall, we were strafed around Saipan one time where some Jap planes came out of nowhere and started shooting at us, missed us.

Q: Do you remember the Marianas "Turkey Shoot?"*

Mr. Bak: That's another area that we were involved in, but that was mostly an air battle. A lot of those planes were coming in, but they were mostly intercepted by our aircraft; some got through.

Q: Was the crew eager for a big battle against the Japanese fleet at that point? I know the officers were.

Mr. Bak: I think we were, considering all of the training for battle that we went through. However, I don't know what we expected as far as what was coming up. As a group we felt very confident because we were in a powerful fleet. You looked out on the horizon and you saw these aircraft carriers, saw all those battleships, and you saw 30 destroyers in a circle. With all this firepower, you felt pretty safe and confident that you could take on anybody. I would have hated like hell to be out by ourselves to face

---
*On 19 June 1944, west of Saipan, U.S. carrier fighters shot down more than 300 Japanese aircraft.

the enemy.

Q: How well were you kept informed on the progress of the war--the island-hopping campaigns and so forth?

Mr. Bak: After every campaign, the captain would give a report on the loudspeaker of what we did. It was after every major engagement that we went into. Sometimes the captain would give us a written report. I know that Captain Stephan gave us a nice letter after we were in the Battle of the Philippine Sea telling exactly what we did, that we were the first team. It was a nice letter that we sent home. My sister gave it, I guess, to a reporter. They put it in the paper, "Mike Bak on the first team." It was kind of a neat thing.

What we in the ship heard did not try to cover things up. If a ship sunk, it was sunk. If we knew the destroyer was one of our squadron, which the Johnston was, why, it was a sad thing to hear.* There was no pussyfooting, no punches being held back. They just told us like it was.

Q: You didn't have that many opportunities to go ashore and blab it to anybody.

---

*The USS Johnston (DD-557), a destroyer in the same division with the Franks, was sunk during the Battle of Leyte Gulf on 25 October 1944, while making courageous attacks against Japanese heavy surface combatants.

Mr. Bak: We were far from anything. In fact, one of the roughest parts out there, I think, was being out at sea for long periods of time--sometimes 30 or 40 days without coming back to port.

Q: At the end of June, Captain Lidstone was relieved, and Captain Stephan came on board.*

Mr. Bak: Yes, he came on board.

Q: What do you recall about the transition? Were you sorry to see Lidstone go?

Mr. Bak: I enjoyed working with Captain Lidstone because I was there every day with him. I almost felt like I knew him very well personally because of being so close to the guy. We were sad to see him go. On the other hand, we accepted whatever came about as just part of the routine. There was a lot of commotion between the crew, "Hey, who's the new captain?" and so forth. "What does he look like?" "I hear he's a bastard." You know, the usual comments. After Captain Lidstone left, everybody said what a fantastic captain he was, more so than when he was there.

Q: What was it about Captain Stephan that made people feel that way about Lidstone in retrospect?

_____
*The change of command was 30 June 1944.

Mr. Bak: In the beginning, all went well. Captain Stephan seemed capable and confident of his abilities. As time went by, some of the crew and officers started calling him a bastard. He was tough and demanding, and he was big. You could sense he was a guy who took command of any situation. He seemed almost like General Patton, that he was born and raised to be a leader in war, and he was loving every part of it. He was in complete charge of that ship. There was no question about it. He was in complete command, whereas Lidstone was very cautious in command. When you saw Stephan with a large group of people, you knew he was the captain. When he was not involved with conning the ship, or not involved with making decisions that affected the entire crew, he was a hell of a nice guy.

I enjoyed Captain Stephan. I never had any problem with him. I thought he didn't care for some of the officers we had aboard our ship. He just felt, in my opinion, that they didn't measure up to his expectations of what an officer should be on board ship. He expected every officer to do the job that he was supposed to be doing. He was demanding. God forbid anybody would be caught sitting in his captain's chair on the bridge when he was supposed to be on watch. Captain Stephan expected the officer of the deck to be out in the front of the bridge instead of inside the charthouse or pilothouse. If it was raining, and many times it was raining out there, and it was wet and nasty, he expected his OOD to be out there. Stephan was not a guy to sit back and relax and take it easy. He was just a guy that was always prepared for any kind of action. That's why I enjoyed the guy. In fact, if I was going to be in the Navy again, I wouldn't mind serving with the guy again, because he seemed to be well trained and thoroughly prepared. He didn't seem to care whether you liked him or not. His main goal seemed to be to impress the fleet commanders and show them he was a capable captain of a destroyer.

Q: How was he toward the enlisted men?

Mr. Bak: He was fair. I think he was much harder on the officers than he was on the enlisted men. I don't think he had too much truck with the enlisted men, other than the people on the bridge, and the fellows in charge of the boatswain's gang, the sea detail, or the radio gang, the communications gang. He was okay with the crew. The biggest problem I think he had was a couple of officers that he didn't get along with. They just hated his guts in some cases. As a general feeling aboard ship the captain was a prick.

Q: Who came to this conclusion and how was it discussed?

Mr. Bak: It was discussed in conversation that led from

things that happened aboard the bridge, where he would be yelling at an officer. It gets around quickly.

Q: So he didn't hesitate to chew them out in front of other people?

Mr. Bak: Well, not generally speaking, but at times he did. You could sense when he was pissed off.

Q: Did he have a short temper?

Mr. Bak: He did with certain people. I know with Lieutenant Numbers he never had a short temper.* I mean, there were guys he respected and he never had a short temper. With Lieutenant Case, I would say, he didn't have a short temper.** Although Lieutenant Case was an uptight guy. He seemed to be almost like Chief Quartermaster Grace in that he was uptight a lot, got angry if things didn't go right. He wanted to make sure nothing screwed up. The captain was a guy that always wanted to know every course change. He was always alert. I mean, you would never see him sleepy, you never would see him tired. He was tired, but he was not a tired tired. When something was happening, he would jump in the scene. He would conn the ship, get out in front of the bridge and make decisions. He was a doer, and a guy that you would like to be a part

---
*Lieutenant (junior grade) Robert E. Numbers, USNR.
**Lieutenant Gerald F. Case, USN.

of, because you know he's a fighter. He's a guy that won't have people working with him that can screw up.

Q: In mess decks did the enlisted men have a tendency to talk about the officers and compare them?

Mr. Bak: Oh, I'm sure we did, yes. I'm sure we did. We all had our favorites as far as officers went. And there were some great guys aboard ship that were really good with the crew. I would say, as a whole, the enlisted men respected the officers we had aboard ship.

Q: Which ones were the favorites?

Mr. Bak: Well, from my standpoint, again, my favorites were fellows like Numbers, Rogers, Meisel, Forer, the navigator.* I was able to be helpful to new officers coming aboard by letting these new officers know the idiosyncrasies of the captain. For example, if I liked the officer real well, I would say, "Look, here's one thing the captain likes. He wants you out there in front of that bridge. When he's in the sack behind the bridge and he gets up, he's going to check on you. So if I were you, I would stay out of the charthouse. Never sit in the captain's chair. Have those binoculars looking around out

---

*Ensign E.J. Rogers, Jr., USNR; Ensign R.K. Meisel, USNR; Lieutenant (junior grade) David Forer, USNR.

there. He's going to come checking on you." And these guys appreciated it, because I gave them straight poop. Most of the officers coming on board had limited or no sea duty.

Q: Of course, it was an opportunity for you not to be so helpful if there was somebody you didn't like.

Mr. Bak: Well, there was one I didn't like. He gave me a bad time one time. We were getting a brand-new ensign on board. In the beginning I didn't like him at all. Later on we became friendly. I was on the quarterdeck watch on one of the islands where we were alongside, I think, a destroyer tender. I guess he didn't like my attitude. I didn't salute him quickly enough probably. I just didn't see him coming. And he said, "Ensign So-and-so reporting for duty." I guess he expected a lot more attention than he got from me at the quarterdeck. Things were more relaxed at anchor than they were under way. Well, later on, I just didn't tell him anything about the captain; he had to learn for himself. When his first shift as junior officer of the deck came around, he was on his own, and the captain chewed him out. But that was the only problem I ever had. Later on, I got to like the guy. He just realized that he'd overreacted. He came to realize that we had been out for many months in the war zone, and you didn't have the formalities out there that you have in a boot camp or other shore areas.

Q: Are there any highlights you recall from the summer of 1944, the period shortly after Commander Stephan took over?

Mr. Bak: One night near Guam, we had three destroyers, one behind the other, conducting night harassing fire. To keep the Japs awake, we were firing 5-inch shells every 20 seconds, salvos into the land. Then we would go down and steam along the island. Then we would come out, circle, and go back around. While we were doing this, a Jap plane came and dropped a bomb in our wake; it just missed us by 50 yards or so. It just brought the whole fantail of the ship up and the bow down. It was one of the smallest planes imaginable; we didn't know where it came from. It came in, dropped the bomb, and took off. We didn't even get a shot at the plane itself. After it hit, we felt like there was a big swell trying to push the ship up out of the water.*

Q: As the fall of 1944 came on, you went to Eniwetok and Espiritu Santo. Did you feel the pace was building up then for the Philippines operation? Were you making preparations for that

---

*The ship's official history indicates that this attack took place on the night of 14 July; the history reports the miss distance as "some 200 yards astern."

Mr. Bak: Well, we always guessed it, because we started looking ahead--where would we strike next? We knew something big was coming up, because there were more and more ships coming out, more and more people. We had already secured a lot of islands, and we were getting closer toward the enemy homeland.

Q: What do you remember about Ulithi as a fleet base?

Mr. Bak: It was very, very big advanced base. We would come in there, and I would imagine it could hold the entire fleet, it was so big. They had a lot of the supply ships and tenders. It was the place where we went back to, to get stores, foods, ammunition, and fuel. We had little liberty in Ulithi that I recall. Maybe we went over on one of the islands and sat under a palm tree with a number on it. Each ship was given a certain number. At the base of the tree you found yourself with six or seven cases of beer, and that was for your crew. You would sit around and drink beer and that was about it, and maybe try to go for a swim. But the coral was so sharp that it would cut your legs up and you couldn't even get in the water. You could wet your toes, but there was no beaches like we have in New Jersey where you could jump in the water and swim around without any danger.

One of the interesting things about Ulithi was that there were so many ships in the fleet coming in that everybody aboard ship had a buddy on another ship. They would come up to the bridge, where the signal gang had a record of the ships in the lagoon. The signalmen always knew, because we had to watch our division commander's mast for signal messages which were given off on the yardarms. And one of the fellows from our crew would come to the bridge and ask if we would call different ships to see if so-and-so was aboard, and maybe get him to talk.

Many times I would give them a light and let people know what ships were in the fleet. Then I would be calling the different ships and asking if Sam Jones was aboard; so-and-so from his hometown was there. He would say, "Yes, we'll get him for you," and then there would be a five- or ten-minute delay, and a flashing light would come back at us. And somebody would say, "This is Sam Jones," and "This is Charlie." They would talk back and forth--"How are you?" They would never see each other, but they would just talk by signal light. It was a highlight of their experience, I would imagine. We did this many times in islands like Ulithi, Manus, and Treasury Islands, where we had fleets where we'd come alongside different ships in an anchorage. In Ulithi sometimes we would be a nest of ships. But most of the time we were anchored out by ourselves.

Q: Then you would ride the boats in to the atoll?

Mr. Bak: Ride the boat. We had one of our whaleboats take

us in.

Q: Well, at least it was a break in the routine.

Mr. Bak: Yes, a break in the routine, but there wasn't a hell of a lot there. The only liberty that I recall--we went to Hollandia one time in New Guinea. We got onto the beach in New Guinea for liberty, and, my God, the only thing we saw--we saw an old lady native who must have been 80 years old and an old man. That was the only natives that we'd seen. It was just desolate. It was just a crappy place to be. It was not clean. It was depressing. So we were happy to get the hell out of there and get back aboard ship.

Q: As the Philippine operation was coming on, you joined the Seventh Fleet.

Mr. Bak: We joined the Seventh Fleet.

Q: What do you remember about the Battle of Leyte Gulf? You touched on it briefly before when you said you saw the ships' masts.

Mr. Bak: That battle I remember very distinctly.* I had just finished eating breakfast, about 7:00 o'clock or 7:15

---

*The battle took place on 25 October 1944.

in the morning, when the loudspeaker announced, "General quarters, general quarters, man your battle stations. Enemy fleet is on the horizon." And we just couldn't believe it. We ran to the battle stations. I ran to the bridge and looked out, and I saw what looked like toothpicks on the horizon, right across the horizon--many, many ships. And our carrier planes started taking off. We were protecting the jeep carriers at that point. I think it was the White Plains, the St. Lo, the Gambier Bay, and we were with a squadron of destroyers. Then the first three destroyers went in for a torpedo run. That was the Johnston and the two other ships that went in there. There were three groups, if I recall, Taffy One, Two, and Three. We were in Taffy Three with our division.* I think Taffy One and Two were the first two groups to go in for the torpedo runs at the Japanese fleet. When the Japanese fleet was coming along at us, our job was to stay between the carriers and the Japanese ships. We were going back and forth, sort of fishtailing because our carriers couldn't go too fast. While we were going back and forth, the Japs were shooting at us and dropping shells around us, 150, 200 yards. When the shells landed, the spots were marked by colored dye. We were going right full rudder, left full rudder, right full rudder, left full rudder, and the shells were coming all around us. Then eventually we

---

*Taffy Three, commanded by Rear Admiral Clifton A.F. Sprague, USN, included the escort carriers Fanshaw Bay (CVE-70), St. Lo (CVE-63), and Gambier Bay (CVE-73), and a screen composed of destroyers and destroyer escorts.

were told to go in for a torpedo run at the Japanese. Finally they decided it was crazy to go in. I think when they found we had lost a couple of ships that were sunk, and we were told to make some smoke screens. So then we laid a smoke screen between the Jap fleet and the jeep carriers. And all the time we did that, we were fishtailing, right full rudder, left full rudder, right full rudder, left full rudder.

Q: Were you on the helm?

Mr. Bak: No, no. I was just at the quartermaster station, putting entries in the ship's log. In fact, I remember this one time when the shells were dropping around us, we didn't know what the hell to do. I was on the bridge. I went under the chart table, which was a ridiculous place to go, but the first class yeoman, a fellow by the name of James Morrison, jumped on top of me. The two of us tried to hide as the shells were dropping around us. I was on a long glass, and I couldn't believe you could see these ships so close. I made out a flag on one of the ships--it was so close. I couldn't believe they go so close to us without our admirals knowing about it. And it was just one of those things that during war everybody is looking the other way, they came in from the rear. It was Kurita's fleet, the Japanese commander involved.*

---
*Vice Admiral Takeo Kurita, Imperial Japanese Navy.

Q: Right.

Mr. Bak: So from about 7:15, 7:20 in the morning until about 10:30, when all this activity was going on, it was just several hours of not knowing what was happening. We did see some burning out there. We thought it was our ships. We didn't know for sure until we got a report later on that was the ships that were sunk. I think the <u>Samuel B. Roberts</u>, the destroyer escort, and the <u>Johnston</u>. Now a quartermaster by the name of Kramer, who was a good friend of mine, was aboard the <u>Johnston</u>. I assume he got killed because most of the fellows were killed in the shelling. We would always pal around with the division quartermasters. When we would nest up, we would just climb on their ship and they would come on ours. We'd look their facilities over, which were the same as ours. You'd just check their neatness versus ours. And then we'd get friendly, just go over some of the things we did.

Q: Were you concerned about your personal safety when all those shells were falling?

Mr. Bak: I was. I would say that was the biggest fear I had in the Navy, because those bastards were shooting pretty good. If we had held one course, I would say they would have blown us out of the water that day. That's what I liked about Stephan.* He was out there giving orders, right full rudder, left full rudder. For some reason or other, later on the Japs turned around and went the other way. They left us when they could have had a kill. They could have just dropped us all, in my opinion. They didn't realize what they had. I believe, reading back in history, they thought that our destroyers were cruisers.

Q: I think Kurita was also concerned about the vast carrier force that Halsey had taken up north, that it might come down.**

Mr. Bak: Yes, yes. That's probably another thing, too. Now the planes were taking off and landing. What I remember an awful lot, too, was getting behind some of these carriers. Some of the pilots went into the water; we were picking them up. So we had the problem of fishtailing and the problem of picking pilots out of the water, because they were landing and taking off regularly. Nobody had any rest. As soon as they landed, they refueled them and got them up again. They put ammunition on them and they would go back up again. We had sort of dual duty, trying to pick

---
*Commander David R. Stephan, USN, commanding officer of the Franks.
**Admiral William F. Halsey, Jr., USN, Commander Third Fleet. Halsey had taken the fast carriers and fast battleships to the north to attack a force of Japanese aircraft carriers. Because he did so, the escort carriers and destroyers had to fend off the large Japanese surface combatants.

our pilots out of the water when they crashed or went overboard, and keeping between the Jap fleet and the escort carriers. But it just seems like the fleet itself was on the other side. The destroyers closest to them were the Johnston and the Hoel.*

Q: How did you feel when they stopped shooting at you?

Mr. Bak: Felt relief. I mean, if was just an amazing thing. But, then again, we heard shortly thereafter that we had lost quite a few ships of the fleet, and in our squadron. So we felt kind of bad. Relief on the one hand, and yet on the other hand you knew you lost guys. You see guys' ships going down. I was on the light, for example, when the St. Lo sent across a message and said that one of the engine rooms was flooded. It was hit; stand by and pick up survivors. The ship was abandoned and later sunk.

Q: Did you see the Gambier Bay sink?

Mr. Bak: Yes. She was with us. I saw the smoke, and I saw her get hit. It was in our formation. The Gambier Bay got hit by Japanese shells. The jeep carriers didn't have the maneuverability we had. That's why they got hit, in my opinion. They got hit because they were slow.

---

*The Hoel (DD-533) and Johnston (DD-557) were sunk during the surface battle.

Q: And they were bigger targets, too.

Mr. Bak: Bigger targets, yes. Well, one of the nice things about being on a destroyer during wartime; they'd go for the big ships first. They didn't bother with destroyers unless we got in their way. Then they started putting shells around us. They were putting shells when we were going in after them for the torpedo run. Then, I guess, we were told to turn around and go back and lay smoke screens instead, because we'd probably get blown out of the water, too. Then the carriers would have been left by themselves and nobody left to protect the carriers. So that's what I think saved our ass as far as the battle. But there was a lot of confusion. I mean, planes all over the place. One of our planes that time actually came down and strafed us--fortunately, he missed us--during that Battle of Leyte Gulf off Samar. I think he just didn't know who the hell was who because of the smoke. And he came down at us and went back up again, and never came back down again. Then the captain gave orders, shoot to kill--anybody that came down on us, shoot. It didn't matter who it was. I think once we may have shot down one of our own guys, just by something like that.

Q: When you're in a battle like that, of course, you can see what's going on, but the people who are below decks can't. Did you have an announcer to tell them?

Mr. Bak: We never gave a running account of what was happening during the actual battle. During general quarters, I made all the announcements. The captain would give results later on, when the battle was all over, for the entire crew. But never during the battle. During general quarters, I made all the announcements. The captain would give results later on, when the battle was all over, for the entire crew. But never during the battle. I felt sorry for those guys being locked down below if we get hit and started to sink.

Q: That would be tough.

Mr. Bak: I think what happened during a battle, the fellows who manned headsets were probably talking and they were telling the guys down below decks what was happening when there wasn't any command from the officer of the deck or the captain to tell them to do something with the engines or something like that.

Q: After the big battle, you moved to carrier operations, and you fairly soon came into the great typhoon of December 1944. What are your recollections of that?

Mr. Bak: It just seemed that we were constantly, in my

opinion, going into the storm. We were being directed by the admiral in charge--Halsey. My recollection is that we were very low on fuel. We tried fueling operations a couple of times, but we couldn't refuel because the weather was so bad. Some of the destroyers were losing their masts and their radars when trying to refuel from a carrier. The mast would bang into the carrier. And it was just a messy thing. With the weather getting worse and worse, the winds getting stronger and stronger, visibility getting very poor, and the waves becoming mountainous. Eventually it got to a point where it got so high that you could not see any ship in the formation. I would say the seas were 80, 90, 100 feet high, and the winds were bad. I saw fellows in the water, but we couldn't help them, because our whaleboats were ripped away. They were washed away, and we had a lot of damage that way. We couldn't steer the ship.

I think we left the screening formation for a while, because at one time the captain wanted to make sure the ship didn't sink. He forgot about the screen and just did everything he possibly could do to keep that ship afloat and trying to head it into the waves. He didn't want to broach. One time I actually was climbing on the outside cabin wall, almost walking on it. We would hang on the outer bulkhead. As the ship was tilting over, we sort of walked up the side of the ship, and then we walked down again and did the other side. I remember distinctly one time where the ship rolled far to the side and stayed there for a full minute without tilting back. It just froze there. We had no idea whether we were going over or not. I was looking around to be in the best position to go overboard. I figured on the bridge was good because that's a high spot. Then the ship would roll back, and it stayed on the other side for about a minute. And then we thought we had it. We didn't know what the hell was going to go on. I was just holding on; everybody was just hanging on. All of a sudden, the ship slowly came back, and we started rolling again.

Q: How far would you guess she rolled over from vertical?

Mr. Bak: I thought we were going to take water into our stacks. That's how far we rolled over. I would say the roll was pretty close to 80 degrees. I really thought we were going to go over. I looked around. Everybody had life preservers on. I always felt if I went over, that I would do okay in the water. I was just so confident I could swim. However, the water was so bad. It was such a bad scene. I don't know how those guys survived that water. I'm glad I was on board a ship and not in the water.

Q: A lot of them didn't.

Mr. Bak: A lot of them didn't. We found out later that

three of the destroyers sank, the Hull, Spence, and the Monaghan. We didn't know that at that time. We were told 62 crew members survived from the Hull, 24 from the Spence, and only six survived from the Monaghan.

Q: Did you actually go alongside another ship and try to refuel?

Mr. Bak: We tried to refuel from the carrier Wasp, but the sea was too rough. But our captain didn't empty his ballast out, because he felt he needed all the weight he could and didn't want to take the chance of being topheavy. Luckily, we were able to hold out.

Q: How long did this period last when the ship was really in the bad part of the storm?

Mr. Bak: I would say we were in there for hours. I honestly believe that we left the screen, and the captain just disregarded all screening responsibilities and just tried to keep the ship afloat. I was on the wheel at one time and I had the wheel at right full rudder, the port engine ahead full, and the starboard back full, and we couldn't make a right turn. We couldn't get out of that position we were in. We just couldn't control the ship. It's the first time I've ever seen a ship of our size that engine power couldn't control it. You just kept it that way until we finally made some headway, and get in the direction we wanted to go. But at this time the captain was always using the engines and the steering wheel to keep the ship afloat constantly. It was emergency full, all speed full, back, reverse engines, and just a constant changing of engines. I think he was always steering with an engine and with the wheel to keep that ship afloat. We didn't see any ships after a while, the visibility was so bad. You could not see the horizon or sky, just swirling water. If you could see 100 yards, or 200 yards, you were lucky. And sometimes you got very close to another ship, and he was trying to prevent it from going over and colliding with us. So it was a very bad scene. It was almost two days, full days, of bad storm. Captain Stephan deserves a lot of credit for pulling us through.

Q: How does life proceed--sleeping and eating?

Mr. Bak: You don't. You stay in your battle stations. I think it was just surviving. Everybody was trying to save his ass, and being somewhere near topside in case we were going over. I don't think anybody was down below, other than the engine room guys and the people who had the watch down below. Everybody else who could be topside--sure, they were topside with their life preservers on. I know we'd walk around and try to get food sometimes. They would have sandwiches and applies. That's the only food we had that we could eat. In those days the storms, even in normal weather where the ship was rolling, you always eat with one hand under the table. As the ship rolls, you pick your rear end up, and you go down. You could look down the whole length of the table and see everybody doing the same motion. That's a common thing. Eating with one hand on a destroyer is common. One hand is always holding on. They had a little lip underneath the table that you held on to, and they had a lip up for your tray to prevent it from sliding off.

Q: You mentioned eating--getting away from the storm for a minute--and the trays. Did you have cafeteria-style serving in your mess deck?

Mr. Bak: Yes, it was cafeteria style. We had a couple cooks behind the counter who were serving food from large pots onto stainless steel trays. The trays were sectioned off to separate different kinds of foods, with the main course having a larger area than the others. You had three openings for food on the tray. Coffee was always served in cups with no handle at all. Handleless cups were easier to stow in the washing machine, to keep them cleaner or whatever. When things got a little bit better, the cooks came around with Spam sandwiches for the crew, the bridge gang, the captain, and the quartermasters, and the signalmen. It would be gobbled up real fast. So that was a neat thing to have the Spam at a time when you were very hungry, and that's all we had, and occasionally apples.

Q: Where would they get the fresh fruit? Was that from the supply ships?

Mr. Bak: Yes, from the supply ships whenever we pulled in to Ulithi or pulled alongside a supply ship or from a destroyer tender. We had refrigeration down below decks, but it just seemed like they held on to those fruits until such time as we used them, and that was the time they came in handy. During the storm, nobody felt like eating at that time. The weather was so bad many of our crew got sick. I think it was just a matter of survival.

Q: Well, I think we've about wrapped up 1944. Why don't we come back next time with '45?

Mr. Bak: Okay. Good deal.

Bak #3 - 168

Interview Number 3 with Michael Bak, Jr.
Place: U.S. Naval Institute, Annapolis, Maryland
Date: Wednesday, 11 June 1986
Interviewer: Paul Stillwell

Q: When you stopped last time--which was two years and two months ago--you had just talked about the typhoon that the Third Fleet went through. Of course, the Franks was part of the Third Fleet. Then you got back to Ulithi about Christmas of 1944.

Mr. Bak: Yes. We got back in to Ulithi, and we tied alongside the destroyer tender USS Piedmont to take on provisions and receive repairs for typhoon damage. While we were tied up alongside the USS Piedmont, I received a copy of their one-page news bulletin dated Tuesday, January 30, 1945. One of the articles was titled "Typhoon Survivors Alongside." It said, "A few weeks ago, the Navy Department announced that one of the worst typhoons in Pacific history had swept over a section of our forces off the east coast of the Philippines, swamping and sinking three of our destroyers. Two of the ships alongside at the present time are survivors of that storm. The 'Fearless' Franks, captained by Comdr. D.R. Stephan, passed right through the center of the blow and escaped to tell about it. The USS Haggard (DD555) under command of Comdr. D.A.

Harris, soon to be relieved by Lt. Comdr. V.J. Soballe, is the second vessel alongside that felt the full fury of the Pacific and came through unscathed. Our hats are off to the officers and men of these two ships for this display of seamanship."

Q: Was there much damage to the <u>Franks</u> as a result of the storm?

Mr. Bak: There was quite a bit of damage. Both whaleboats washed away, stripped from the mooring, and we had some topside damage. I don't recall any structural damage. The waves were coming over the bridge and sometimes over the stacks, and I don't know whether we had damage to the engine room. I believe some of our life rafts disappeared along with the whaleboats.

Q: This was another year that you were away from home, having to spend the holidays separated from your family. What was the feeling?

Mr. Bak: When you have time to relax, you think about home and what you would have been doing if you were there, and wondering about when the war might be over. Sitting down and just having a lot of conversations with friends of yours aboard ship. Once in a while, I played my harmonica for whomever would want to listen. Sometimes I would spend time identifying stars for some of the sailors who would see some bright constellations and wonder what they were, or maybe settle a few bets on what the stars were. One of my hobbies during the Navy days was to study the stars, because I was involved in taking a lot of sights for the navigator.

Q: You had expressed to me earlier the idea that you were going to get in, do your service, win the war, and get home. Did you have an idea by this time, at the beginning of 1945, how much longer it might take?

Mr. Bak: Well, we didn't have any idea, but we thought it would take much longer than when the war abruptly ended. We just felt it was going to be a long haul--just a discussion about the length of time it would take for the Army and the Marines to mop up once they had landed on the home islands. I didn't know, and I don't think anybody aboard ship had any feeling, other than it was going to be a long, drawn-out war.

Q: Just a day-to-day thing.

Mr. Bak: It was a day-to-day thing, and also a feeling that we were lucky so far, and we hoped that the luck would hold out, that we would not get hurt, or not get sunk.

Q: You mentioned the Allies. Was there any discussion about the British role and a possible Russian role?

Mr. Bak: No. The only news we ever had was the captain would occasionally announce some major event that was happening. If there was a battle in Europe or a landing was made, the captain would receive some information and just over the loudspeaker would give a capsule type of a quick news report to the crew. If we lost some ships, they would definitely tell us we lost a ship, the names of the ships, and how many men were reported missing. The area of losses was never held back. It just seemed that we accepted whatever he told us, and we went on about our duty; nobody complained. It was just a feeling of "Let's get the job done."

Q: Now, is this Captain Stephan you're speaking of, that made the announcements?

Mr. Bak: Yes, Captain Stephan.* He was good about giving information. I remember two or three times we received a one-page or a two-page single-space letter describing the activities. After we were in an engagement, he would give a report of the action of the USS Franks crew. Each of us got a copy, and we would send it home to the folks back home, proud of our accomplishments.

---
*Commander David R. Stephan, USN, was commanding officer of the USS Franks (DD-554) from 30 June 1944 to 2 April 1945.

Q: That's sort of what's known as a family-gram now.

Mr. Bak: A family-gram now, yes. Captain Stephan was a good guy and seemed to know what he was doing; he was always on the alert. When things were quiet, between operations, he'd run the ship with a pipe in his hand and just be very pleasant. But once we'd get going and once things were happening, he became a different personality; he became all business and didn't waste a minute relaxing.

Q: He probably lived on the bridge, practically.

Mr. Bak: Lived on the bridge, practically. He had that small captain's sea cabin, just back of the bridge itself. Every once in a while, I remember him coming out in his shorts. It was warm, and he was just walking around to see how things were going, if he couldn't sleep, or if he was reading in his cabin. Or if the officer of the deck would give him a report of any kind of change out of the ordinary that occurred, he had to be notified. Or the quartermaster on watch would notify him and give him a message from the officer of the deck.

Q: Do you remember anything specific with the destroyer tender that you were alongside? Did she provide any services to your ship?

Mr. Bak: The various divisions aboard our ship always had a list of things they needed. Our shipfitters always got the supplies they needed; our machinists received machine tools that they needed; the quartermaster gang picked up new charts that we needed; the signal gang got binoculars. I remember one time I lost a long glass. I was sitting on the signal bridge spotlight platform when a long glass slipped right through my hand during a heavy storm and heavy waves. The tenders also provided movies to the supply officer. Every time we pulled into port somewhere, the crew was always loading ammunition, it seems, and always loading provisions and stores. In these instances all hands were involved.

Q: Did you load ammunition under way at all?

Mr. Bak: We might have loaded ammunition under way a couple of times. In one period, we were at sea maybe three or four weeks, where we did an awful lot of shooting. I believe we loaded ammunition under way, but I'm not sure. Loading ammunition while under way could prove very dangerous.

Q: It sounds as if it was infrequent, though, under way.

Mr. Bak: It was mostly, I would say, at port where we were next to an ammunition ship, and we had long lines of fellows passing ammunition over.

Q: One advantage for you as a senior petty officer is that you didn't have to get involved in a lot of those working parties.

Mr. Bak: That's not true. On a destroyer it wasn't true.

Q: Oh, really?

Mr. Bak: Not on the destroyer that I was on, anyway; we didn't have that many crew members. Each of us pitched in. If we were off duty, we pitched in. We did get away with some of the things, but when all hands were required, everybody pitched in.

Q: How big a role did religion play in the life of the ship?

Mr. Bak: We occasionally had religious services aboard our ship. The only religious services that I attended were when we were at anchor and it happened to be a Sunday. I remember going over oftentimes to an aircraft carrier and listening to a sermon. I would sit on a bench on the flight deck and get goosebumps whenever I'd hear the song

"Eternal Father, strong to save."* The wording of that hymn was so apropros of what we were always doing.

We didn't have a chaplain aboard ship. When we went alongside a destroyer tender, if it was Sunday, they always announced church services, and you were welcome to attend. I was brought up with a father who was in church every Sunday and had us go every Sunday. As a result, why--that was the only time religion played a part, other than our own individual devotions to the Almighty, as far as whatever way we did it in our own being.

Q: Did they have any lay leaders at all on board your ship?

Mr. Bak: Not to my knowledge, no organized lay leaders at all.

Q: I would be surprised if they had a chaplain as specialized as Russian Orthodox. How did you fall in on a denomination?

Mr. Bak: I always went to the Protestant services, which is close to our religion. It was something that I could understand. Being a Greek Orthodox with a Russian background and going to church where all the services were in Russian, I was never really able to comprehend what was

---
*These are the opening words of the Navy Hymn.

being said and what was being done. But I did go, and I just did know that it was the thing to do. So I always felt that if I could understand what was happening, I would go to the Presbyterian services. It was kind of a neat thing, to get up and be up on a carrier deck, getting over by whaleboat, climbing and just seeing this big awesome ship. We didn't get too many opportunities to visit, other than church services or playing basketball. That was the only time I was ever on an aircraft carrier. The other time I did, when I took for my examinations for--I think it was for the V-5 program, for the Navy flight program. That was the only time that I was ever physically on an aircraft carrier during my times in the service.

Q: You got under way then in early 1945, and you were with Task Group 38.2. I wonder if you have any recollections about working with the carriers at night.

Mr. Bak: We were part of Task Force 38's night flying carrier task group, consisting of the USS Enterprise and the USS Independence. Two destroyer divisions were assigned to screen the carriers: DesDiv 93--McCord, Hazelwood, and Trathen; DesDiv 94 consisting of the Franks, Haggard, and Buchanan. Our mission was to improve and extend night search and introduce night striking. However, during the daylight we operated within the screen of Task Group 38.2 under Rear Admiral Bogan.* At night we could

---

*Rear Admiral Gerald F. Bogan, USN, whose oral history is in the Naval Institute collection.

just see faintly the lights of the carrier decks that were lit up when the planes were taking off. We had an excellent view in the position of a plane guard ship. The <u>Franks</u> left the screening formation and got behind the carriers to pick up pilots if they landed in the ocean. It was a nice feeling to watch those planes take off. You saw the flame of an airplane engine as it took off the carrier deck; you could see that light, and then it disappeared into the darkness. They had some accidents where planes went over the side or crashed into the water or were shot up and had difficulty landing on an aircraft carrier.

Q: Did you have to make any of those pickups at night?

Mr. Bak: Yes. The light attached to the Mae West life jacket saved one of the pilots that went down into the water, and the water was very rough.* When the pilot came on board, he was delirious and half drowned. When he later felt better, he asked about his gun, and they said it disappeared; it probably was sunk. Ensign O'Neill was the one that actually picked up the .45 as a souvenir of the pilot who went down into the water.** Anyway, that was

---

*"Mae West" was the nickname for a type of life jacket, because when it was inflated the wearer's chest bore some resemblance to that of the buxom movie actress of the time. The life jackets were equipped with police whistles and small flashlights to attract the attention of passing ships at night.
**Ensign John H. O'Neill, USNR.

the story O'Neill told at the reunion that we had in San Antonio.

So when the pilots came on board, they were so appreciative of being saved by the crew, that the officers had first crack at getting souvenirs, which we enlisted men didn't know about until after it was all over. The doctor would probably be the first one to minister to the pilot, and then the officers would be next in line to visit. If the pilot was in pretty good shape, they could talk. It might be a day or two before he was sent back to his carrier by breeches buoy.

Q: He had been picked clean by then.

Mr. Bak: Picked clean by then.

Q: Of course, he wouldn't have to account for anything. He could say it was lost in the crash.

Mr. Bak: He wouldn't have to account for it. He was happy to be alive. And I'm sure the admiral aboard the carrier was happy to have him safely returned. I've got some nice pictures that were taken by our ship's official photographer, Gaylord S. Johnson, a series of pictures from the time we picked the pilot out of the water and when we transferred him by breeches buoy.

Q: Was there a tradition that the carrier would send over some ice cream as a reward?

Mr. Bak: Yes. The tradition was every time we sent a pilot back via the breeches buoy, they would load a 15-gallon drum of ice cream on return. It was enough ice cream for the entire crew. It was a treat and a high point of the next meal. One of the reasons our crew really went all out to pick up the pilots out of the water was to get the ice cream, which was rare for us in the Navy. We had no ice cream-making machines aboard our ship, and it was a tribute to our sailors who went into the water to rescue the pilots.

From my standpoint, being on the bridge right next to the captain and the officer of the deck always, I had a first row seat for watching the entire proceedings. In other words, if I had been a gunner or in another part of the ship on duty, I would never have seen all of the activity taking place to pick up the pilot out of the water. The captain always had the best position to see what was going on, and I was always nearby.

Q: How long would a pilot stay on board the _Franks_ after he was picked up?

Mr. Bak: Depending upon his condition and what our

function was in the fleet operations. The weather had to be good, and depending upon where they were going. I would say a day or two maximum, depending on how badly he was hurt. Like, sometimes, the guy had a big gash on his head, and you could see his face was half torn off. He would probably be on board for a while. And mainly depending upon the conditions at sea. Now there was a thing among carrier pilots; they were fearful sometimes getting transferred after pickup from a destroyer to an aircraft carrier. Because there were some rumors that some of the destroyers in the fleet had problems where either the line snapped when they were transported across, or the two ships came close together where the guy almost drowned. We never had that happen aboard our ship. I've never seen that happen, because I was on the bridge every transfer. We picked up 22 carrier pilots out of the water, and we returned 22 pilots. Our crew handling the transfers did an excellent job. We never had a problem. I do know that was a fear on the part of some pilots.

Q: I think that's a natural reaction when you're suspended over the water.

Mr. Bak: One of the things we noticed on an aircraft carrier was that whenever a pilot was transferred back to his ship, the deck was always lined with his flying buddies. I mean, you would see 30, 40, 50 pilots out there on top of the deck, cheering their buddy as he was returning back to the ship. There was always a large number of people watching the seamanship between ships getting this pilot back--the rigging up of the breeches buoy and making sure the lines were taut. I handled the helm on several occasions when pilots were returned to their carriers.

Q: Did you transfer people like that other than pilots?

Mr. Bak: We did. I think we had a sick person once, the fellow who was seasick. We may have done it once or twice. But not very often, not very often.

Q: How good was the medical care aboard ship, both for treating pilots and in general?

Mr. Bak: Well, we had a medical doctor aboard our ship, a full-fledged doctor. He was, I understand, pretty good. He'd patch these pilots up very well. In fact, Ernie Pyle wrote a very nice article about our ship in one of the magazines complimenting the treatment received by the carrier pilot when he was aboard our ship.* Patched them up pretty well.

---

*Pyle was a nationally known newspaper correspondent. He had made a name for himself by reporting on enlisted soldiers in the European theater. He transferred to the Pacific near the end of the war. He was killed during the Okinawa campaign.

Q: Was Pyle on board the *Franks*?

Mr. Bak: No, he was never on board the *Franks*. Evidently, he was on one of the carriers where we picked up a pilot and he interviewed that pilot when he got back in, and asked him about what happened and so forth. He described his events of what happened aboard ship. After the war, I received a copy of Ernie Pyle's article about this occasion. I still have it. It was called "Retrievers of Ditched Pilots." The pilot was Jimmy Van Fleet of Findlay, Ohio.

Q: Was there much occasion for the doctor to do things other than that? I mean, you've got young men that are generally healthy.

Mr. Bak: Well, yes. He prescribed the usual pills if people got sick. Usually colds or something like that. I don't recall anybody breaking their bones or getting injured. We may have had one appendicitis attack or something. But I don't remember any major surgery being performed. Although the doctor was capable of handling surgery on a limited basis, he, to my knowledge, never was called upon to demonstrate his talents.

Q: During this period of early January, you were

supporting air strikes on Formosa and the island of Luzon in the Philippines. Do you have any recollection of the amount of enemy aircraft?

Mr. Bak: Yes. I remember we went between the Philippine Islands and Formosa. The first time we went out, we went out with a large fleet of ships. We were headed for the South China Sea through the Luzon Strait. The Japanese came up with air strikes, and we had a lot of planes up in the air. Our planes shot down three Japanese planes, and there was a lot of ack-ack. The whole sky seemed to be filled with black pockmarks from the 5-inch guns; everybody was firing. Our carrier planes made strikes over the airfields on the China coast. We lost 12 carrier planes while our pilots got 16 Jap planes in the air and 18 more on the ground. During an 11-day period, the Third Fleet logged 3,800 miles in the South China Sea without incurring a serious mishap.

I remember coming back several days later through the same strait; we had an even greater amount of Japanese planes attacking the fleet. It seemed like they all came out, and they were waiting for the fleet to come back through Luzon Strait. I think that period of time was the greatest concentration of aircraft and firepower by our Navy ships during my time in the _Franks_. It was the first time that the fleet seemed to go out that far west.

Q: Did you feel an increased sense of danger as you got closer to the Japanese homeland?

Mr. Bak: We knew we were going to have a lot of activity, but I always felt secure in knowing that we had a good crew and a good captain. I always felt in my heart that, "We're going to survive, no matter what." We were lucky. I was very confident of coming back, although I was afraid many times. Most of the crew felt that way, too, because we were all a bunch of young fellows, early 20s. It's like being in a theater watching a war going on, but you're participating instead of just watching it.

Q: I suppose it's something like the mechanism when you go out driving a car; you figure there are accidents, sure, but they'll happen to other people.

Mr. Bak: That's exactly the way you look at that feeling. I felt secure because whenever we had an air attack the Japanese aircraft rarely went after the destroyers. When they attacked the fleet, they always went after the aircraft carriers. We could watch them going down, diving down at the aircraft carriers as our guns were shooting at them. Then if they were actually shot up and were losing altitude, they would try to crash into the nearest ship. All we had to do was shoot at them and hope they wouldn't crash into us. About the only fear we had was when we were from the fleet, and trying to get radar information of the approaching enemy aircraft. Being there by yourself and being attacked by a Japanese plane--that would be the biggest fear I had, I would say, in the Navy. Fortunately, most of the times that we had picket duty, we had overcast skies and we knew a lot of Jap planes were above us. We knew that we would have been attacked had we not had the cloud covering. We knew, by radar, they were up there.

Q: That was probably later, up around Okinawa, wasn't it?

Mr. Bak: That was later on; you're right. That was in Okinawa. At this time we were with Task Group 38.2.

Q: Did you have a concern about submarines at this point early in '45?

Mr. Bak: The submarines at this point in the war seemed to be less and less, to my way of thinking, of a threat to our fleet, although our main concern, as a destroyer, was to be in a screen, to watch out for submarines. But it just seems that we didn't get as many contacts as we did in the first part of the war.

Q: During that time you were in the South China Sea, you

were with Halsey.* And I think he was particularly interested in getting the two battleship conversions--the *Ise* and the *Hyuga*--that he had missed at Leyte Gulf. What do you remember about that particular operation? This would have been in between the two times that you went through that passage, because you went down into the South China Sea and were there for a while, then came back out.

Mr. Bak: We bombarded the China coast; we bombarded, I believe it was Hong Kong, as I recall. It was nice to see the China coast in the distance, but we were never on China itself. We did see it and we did bombard it, but we never did encounter any Japanese large fleet. I think at the time we were there, we might have hit some barges or some small craft.

Q: Was Halsey's presence felt at your ship level?

Mr. Bak: Oh, yes, because we could see him on the battleship *New Jersey* when we refueled at sea. He'd be sitting up there on the bridge, you know, looking around and wearing his cap. Everybody pointed, "There's Bull Halsey." When we were refueling 60 feet away from the battleship *New Jersey*, it was just kind of a neat feeling to know that the main fleet commander of the Pacific war was right next to you, and you were part of that fleet.

---
*Admiral William F. Halsey, Jr., USN, Commander Third Fleet.

And the other thing--the ship's crew was allowed to listen to radio broadcasts at certain times when Tokyo Rose would give out different reports of sinkings. I believe the <u>Franks</u> was reported sunk three times by Tokyo Rose.* They mistook us several times for a cruiser.

Q: Was that a source of amusement on board?

Mr. Bak: It was a source of amusement, and it was a great therapy for us, because Tokyo Rose was a symbol. I remember one specific time, and I wrote it down in my diary, which I still have, when Tokyo Rose announced, "Tens of thousands of the flower of American youth will perish to Davy Jones' locker shortly."** Everybody cracked up laughing.

Q: During the month of February 1945, you got into the Iwo Jima operation and the first strikes against the Japanese homeland. What do you remember about those operations?

Mr. Bak: Prior to the Iwo Jima invasion, the <u>Franks</u> was one of five destroyers assigned to scouting patrols ahead

---

*"Tokyo Rose" was the nickname of Iva Ikuko Toguri D'Aquino, an American citizen born of Japanese parents. Her English-language radio broadcasts from Japan were intended to demoralize the U.S. fighting men who heard them. In fact, many servicemen found them a source of amusement because of the greatly exaggerated claims of American losses.
**This quotation is from Mr. Bak's diary entry of 14 October 1944.

of carriers on the way to bomb Tokyo and Honshu. Then we returned to the Iwo Jima area, where our carrier planes struck targets, damaging a number of gun positions. We also went in with the battleships to bombard the island of Iwo Jima. Usually the battleships went in first during daylight hours and heavily bombard the island, and then we would go in at nighttime to bombard the island from about a mile or two away. We occasionally got shot at by the Japanese, and shrapnel fell on the ship. We never had any damage. We had a job of softening up the island of Iwo Jima.

Q: What was your role as a quartermaster in shore bombardment, say, at Iwo Jima?

Mr. Bak: Primarily recording the action in the log. My role was basically assistant to the navigator and the officer of the deck. I would be on the pelorus stand and taking tangents, the right and left tangent of the island. The navigator would give the information to combat information center; the combat information center would then give the information to the gunnery offices, and they would aim their guns and fire at certain targets on land.

Each ship had target areas to shoot at. Each ship had grid charts showing the island, and each chart showed squares designated by letters and numbers. Spotters called with specific targets to shoot at.

Q: It's important to fix the position of the ship accurately so you know the correct azimuth to fire to hit that point on land.

Mr. Bak: Accuracy was very important. The navigator was always very busy in his giving position reports to the gunnery officers and yelling down into the tubes to CIC. They would be plotting the same plot on their CIC scope and their charts, as well as the navigator up above.

So we would bombard. I remember distinctly that we had a hospital corpsman, before actual bombardment took place, distribute cotton to the crew. We would stuff cotton into our ears for protection. Every time we fired those guns, there was a tremendous noise. I think in the Battle of Iwo Jima, we fired many rounds and it was very noisy. There's no place to go aboard ship that you wouldn't get noise, because the 5-inch guns were situated with two forward and three aft. Boy, when those guns forward fired, and they were just so close to the bridge--they were pointing at a horizontal level toward the land at a 90-degree angle from the bridge. That smoke sometimes came right toward the bridge, and if the wind was right, we'd get some of the debris and smell the smoke and hear the noise. The noise was the worst part of the shelling.

Q: You finished up that operation, back to Ulithi, and

then out again with the carriers, this time supporting strikes on Kyushu. I wonder if there is anything to differentiate that operation from the ones before and after. By then it was March 1945.

Mr. Bak: We spent the first two weeks of that month in Ulithi. We were able to go ashore, drink beer, and swim. We also swam off the port side of the ship during this period. It was a period of relaxation, movies, and even had a chance to play basketball against some carrier teams that were in the lagoon. As we left Ulithi, we did a lot of plane guard duty between the Yorktown and the Enterprise. Heavy Jap bomber attacks started on the fleet, aiming for the carriers. A couple of Jap pilots parachuted after being hit. Someone in our fleet opened up on the floating airmen. During this action, the USS Franklin got hit.* I watched planes with shot-up landing gear trying to land and pilots who crashed and drowned before we could reach them. During this action, I was able to listen to the radio conversations between the ships.

That was one of the things I enjoyed a lot, being on the bridge, was to hear what was going on. Any activity that was reported to the captain, I knew firsthand because I was there, on the bridge itself. The only other people on the bridge would be, maybe, the officer of the deck, the junior

---

*On 19 March 1945, the carrier Franklin (CV-13) was hit by two enemy bombs while operating off Japan. Altogether 724 men were killed and 265 wounded.

officer of the deck, the helmsman, myself, maybe a torpedoman who would be near the bridge with his earphones and ready to take any action as far as torpedoes were concerned. And that was about it. So you didn't have a lot of people listening to the conversation. We had occasionally the first class yeoman who was standing by up there as a phone talker for the captain. It just seemed that some of the first class petty officers always were hanging around the bridge to see what was going on.

Q: You probably had a boatswain's mate of the watch and some lookouts.

Mr. Bak: Yes, we had two lookouts--one port and starboard. Then we had a signal watch, but they were always behind the bridge. They would walk forward once in a while and shoot the breeze. That's my recollection of Honshu. We were told we were preparing for a big strike, and we felt ready. Just about this time, it could have been one of the first times we saw B-29s coming over our fleet, and we saw many, many B-29s--they filled the whole sky--and started going toward Japan. It was just an awesome, awesome sight. That's why we had no fear. That's why we thought maybe, seeing those planes going toward Japan that the war would be ended sooner. I never heard of a B-29 until we first saw them in the sky and it was a nice feeling.

Q: Also, then, on the 24th of March, you were with a group of battleships that bombarded Okinawa. That must have been an impressive sight also.

Mr. Bak: That was the most firepower, probably, that we were involved in on a steady basis. It just seemed like we did an awful lot of bombarding of Okinawa. We were screening the battleships during the daytime. A total of three battleships were in our group: New Jersey, Wisconsin, and Missouri. They were just sort of lined up off the beach, maybe 3 or 4 or 5 miles maximum, just pointing their guns toward Okinawa, and all day long just bombarded away. You'd see those big flames coming out of the guns and the tremendous noise.

Then at nighttime, along with three other destroyers, we were in for harassing fire, up and down, one destroyer after another, and just firing away, every 20 seconds, 5-inch salvos. Then making a circle and then coming back around and starting the same pattern, while the destroyers behind us were doing the same thing. We were told it was to keep the Japs awake.

Q: Did it keep the people in your ship awake when you were trying to sleep?

Mr. Bak: You couldn't sleep, because the crew was at general quarters. We were up all night for two or three nights in a row.

Q: You mentioned the New Jersey. A couple of weeks later, on the second of April, you were in Task Group 58.4, plane-guarding for the Yorktown, and then had a collision with the New Jersey. Could you describe the events of the collision, please?

Mr. Bak: I remember distinctly it was a very dark night, and the weather was not good at all.* There was a little rain, overcast, and visibility was very poor. We were conducting night fighter flight operations, and were screening the carriers. At the start of flight operations, we left our screen station to proceed behind the carrier Yorktown. I went off duty at 8:00 o'clock and went down to my bunk. Bill Middleton, our second class quartermaster, relieved me to take over the 8:00 to 12:00 watch. About 9:15 we were just finished night fighter operations and were proceeding back to the screen. I was down below decks when it seemed like we hit something, but I didn't know what it was. It was a sudden jolt. I thought we had hit a mine in the forward part of the ship, because I was in the after compartment, and all the lights went out; the ship rolled back and forth. I was in my shorts. I quickly jumped out of the sack and made way for the deck--figuring

---

*For more on this collision of 2 April 1945, see Paul Stillwell, Battleship New Jersey: An Illustrated History (Annapolis: Naval Institute Press, 1986), pages 77-78.

that we were going to be going overboard. I believe I was the first one out of the compartment, even though I wasn't the closest to the hatch. I knew every step of the way. I went up topside, and I would say we were rolling about 20-25 degrees. It was cold as heck, and I was ready to go over the side, but I felt we were okay; we were not sinking. There was a lot of noise, a lot of fellows running and yelling.

Then I made my way up the starboard side of the ship and didn't see any damage. When I got to the bridge, at my station, my God, half the port side of the bridge was sliced away; it was just split. And I was told that we had a collision with the battleship New Jersey.

Q: Could you see her at all?

Mr. Bak: No, the battleship was gone. One of the officers saw me in my shorts and bare feet. He lent me a winter parka with a fur lining. I used that for a while and it was very warm, and I felt very comfortable. At that time we were told to stay away from the port side of the bridge because the port wing of the bridge was gone. If you just sort of stuck your head back, you could see part of the stacks; the upper structure of the ship was damaged. Then we heard that the captain was down below and he was hurt, and that Numbers was hurt.*

---
*Lieutenant (junior grade) Robert E. Numbers, USNR.

Jack Dillon was a signalman; he was stunned and hurt.*
He fell down below, on a potato locker, when the signal
bridge on the port side was pretty well severed. It was
just like a knife going through at a 45-degree angle above
the bridge itself. It just ripped the entire port side of
the ship. The anchor of the New Jersey did the damage to
our destroyer, and because the anchor was so high off the
water, it hit our destroyer, and that was the reason why we
weren't hit or damaged below decks, and that's the reason
why we didn't sink, as well. It just seemed when I was
down below decks, before the actual collision, that the
ship actually stopped for a while, for some reason or
other. We were in the water proceeding, and we would
usually do around 10 or 15 knots when maneuvering in and
out of ships, that the ship stopped and all of a sudden
started again.

From the reports that I got from some of my crew
members, we missed the Yorktown by inches. When we were
leaving the formation of plane guard, evidently there must
have been a maneuvering board problem error in the
direction the ship was supposed to leave to go to its new
location in the screen. We'd been doing this maneuver for
a long time, since the start of the first campaign at
Gilbert Islands, when we were plane guard ship for the
Liscome Bay, and this was quite a bit later. We were an
experienced plane guard ship. We had some close calls, but

───────────
*Signalman Jackie N. Dillon.

we never had a real close call as this one here. So I don't know what happened or whose fault it was, whether it was the battleship New Jersey's or whether it was the Franks's. It was just an accident that happened at sea. The weather was lousy. It happened so fast.

Q: What happened in the immediate aftermath, as you were recovering from this?

Mr. Bak: After the immediate aftermath, the captain was transported, I believe, to an oil tanker that was part of the fleet for additional medical attention. We knew the captain was critically injured; he had some ribs broken into his lungs.

He died about a day or two later, and I recall leaving our ship in a whaleboat with Lieutenant Case and two or three other members of our crew to go to the tanker to attend the funeral services of Captain Stephan.* I distinctly remember standing on the deck, and the crew of the tanker had a platform that was extending over the side of the ship. The platform had Captain Stephan's body encased in a canvas bag that had a lot of weights attached to it. Draped over the canvas bag was the American flag. Then, after a brief ceremony and eulogy, they just raised the rear of the platform, and the body slid into the water

---

*Lieutenant Gerald F. Case, USN, succeeded to command when Commander Stephan was injured.

and disappeared. Then we returned by whaleboat to our ship.

Q: What were your emotions at that point, in having lost your captain?

Mr. Bak: It was very sad, because I personally was very fond of the captain, even though a lot of people didn't like him. I was one of the few enlisted men aboard ship who really was close to the captain because of my quartermaster rating. Paul Green, our second class signalman, and I always stood up for the captain. It was an eerie feeling to see a body draped on a slab one moment and the next disappearing over the side. I felt very sad and helpless to see a man that I admired end his career in this fashion: a collision at sea with one of our own ships, instead of dying as a result of enemy action. When the ceremony ended, it was very quiet. When the members of our party climbed aboard our whaleboat to return to the ship, no one spoke. This was the only burial at sea that I witnessed. I know many of our crew never shed a tear when he died. A good number of them were glad he was no longer with us. I also personally believe that the captain's evasive action to avoid a collision saved the entire crew from either being killed or drowned. No one ever gave him credit for saving the ship from sinking. He remained at his post shouting commands until the time of impact.

Ironically, he was the only one killed. The entire crew survived with only a few casualties.

Q: Was he tough on the crew?

Mr. Bak: He was tough on the crew, especially if you screwed up, and a lot of people didn't like him because of that. He always looked for perfection. A lot of them called him a bastard. But those of us on the bridge, like the signal gang and the quartermaster gang, didn't have the same feeling toward the captain that most of the other crew members had. I believe a lot of the stories about the captain came from some of the officers aboard ship who were officers of the deck, and he may have been hard on them, for whatever reasons. Maybe they didn't measure up to his expectations, or maybe something happened in the wardroom, or personality clashes; I don't know what the situation was. But it seemed that some of the crew members unjustly criticized him for some of the things he was accused of.

Q: I think a difference might have been that you knew of him as a person, and they had only heard about him.

Mr. Bak: They only heard about him, and they'd see him at certain times. A lot of the crew members were rarely on the bridge under way, because that was not their station. So I think a lot of those stories that circulated about

Captain Stephan were circulated by some of the officers who really hated him with a passion. One of the officers, I thought, wanted to shoot him with a .45.

Q: This is Lieutenant Commander Crabbe?

Mr. Bak: Yes. When we left Ulithi in the middle of March, heading for strikes against Kyushu, Japan, our executive officer, Lieutenant Commander C.R. Crabbe, USNR, disappeared from our ship. When I went down one time to wake him up for star sights, he was sleeping with a .45 on his chest. I reported it to the captain. I thought probably he was going to shoot himself or somebody else aboard ship.

On the day of his disappearance, I was also supposed to wake him up for star sights. However, he was nowhere to be found. A search of the ship was organized without success. We couldn't find any trace of him. We didn't know for sure what had happened. Some people thought he might have fallen overboard; others thought he might have been pushed or have gone over on his own. Much to our surprise, about an hour later, a destroyer in the stern of our formation, the USS Scott, sent a TBS (talk between ships) message saying that they picked up Lieutenant Commander Crabbe out of the water. We were all shocked when we heard the message. The executive officer was lucky that the Franks was in the forward part of the formation. My own personal feeling is that he jumped overboard trying to commit suicide. The cold water must have given him second thoughts. Captain Stephan and the lieutenant commander never got along. Subsequent, Lieutenant Commander Crabbe was transferred from the <u>Scott</u> to another ship in the fleet, and we never heard from him after that.

So far as the captain goes and that day that he died, I liked the guy. I wouldn't mind serving anywhere in any kind of a battle action with him, because I thought he was very competent. I thought he was more sure of himself than Captain Lidstone, although Captain Lidstone was a very nice, efficient officer.* He was a conservative, competent officer. I think Captain Stephan was looking for ways to really do the job better. Whatever assignment that he was given, whatever the commander of the task force gave to the <u>Franks</u> to do, he immediately got the officers together, got everybody together, "We're going to do this, and we're going to do that." And we'd take off.

Q: You could argue that it would have been better to have a conservative man during that night rather than somebody who was impulsive.

Mr. Bak: That could be. That could be. However, on the other hand, I don't know--so many times I would prefer to

---

*Commander Nicholas A. Lidstone, USN, was commanding officer of the <u>Franks</u> from the time of her commissioning to 30 June 1944.

be with Stephan; that's my own feeling, maybe because we had more action with Stephan than we did with Lidstone.

Q: What impressions did you have of Lieutenant Case during the brief time he was in command?

Mr. Bak: Lieutenant Case was the engineering officer. Lieutenant Case seemed to me a very uptight officer. He wasn't in the class of Lidstone or Stephan. To me he was not as sure of himself as the other fellows. But when he did take command, you could tell he enjoyed being the captain. He did a good job of bringing us back safely to Ulithi.

Lieutenant Case seemed to keep to himself and be very quiet. I would say he was an introvert. He would just seem to be not as friendly a person as some of the other officers. He would just sort of walk back and forth on the bridge, just couldn't sit still, looking around, probably because he didn't spend too much time as officer of the deck. I never remember him being an easy guy to sit down and shoot the breeze with like I was able with the navigator and some of the other officers. Maybe I'm judging him wrong, but that was my own personal feeling. He did a good job of getting the ship back. He seemed to take command and knew what he was doing. He relied on the navigator an awful lot.

Q: In fairness to him, you couldn't put him in a category with Lidstone or Stephan, because he just didn't have that much experience.

Mr. Bak: That would be another reason, too. That would probably be it, because the running of the ship itself, the routine of running the ship, was not his bag. He was the engineering officer.* He didn't know the routine of running the ship, and I think he relied on everybody aboard, and rightfully so. He just took over command. He was senior officer present aboard the ship at the time, and he took us back. He relied on everybody else, so everybody aboard the ship itself seemed to do the duty they were supposed to do, and the ship got back safely. He conned the ship to Ulithi and then brought us back to Pearl Harbor.**

Q: You went alongside a tender for a while there at Ulithi. What happened during that period to get you squared away?

Mr. Bak: I remember we had temporary repairs to fix whatever damage and whatever listing we had aboard the ship. A lot of the things that were going on, I was not

---
*Lieutenant Case had become the acting executive officer upon the disappearance of Lieutenant Commander Crabbe.
**The Franks arrived at Pearl Harbor on 21 April 1945; on 22 April, Lieutenant Commander Eugene B. Henry, Jr., USN, took over command from Case.

aware of at Ulithi. I know we had workmen coming back and forth, and we were taking on provisions while waiting for news of what was going to happen next. At that point, we didn't know where we would be going. I don't remember when they actually gave us that instruction to go back to the States. Other than getting food and provisions, there was not much, to my opinion, that actually happened, other than people who were aboard that ship or personnel from other ships in the fleet would come by and see our ship damage and wonder what happened.

Q: Did any come over to visit and ask questions?

Mr. Bak: It appeared that we had some visitors aboard, yes, to see what the actual damage was. We always had a certain amount of people, not too many, just go back and forth. Since we were next to the tender itself, we would have access to visit the tender. I think a lot of our different divisions on the ship used that opportunity to pick up some stuff that was probably missing or maybe pilfered and say it went over the side.

Q: Were these just emergency repairs at Ulithi

Mr. Bak: I would say they were emergency repairs only. There was nothing big of any kind. I think they wanted to make sure that the ship was seaworthy to get us back safely to Pearl Harbor. And it seemed when we left Ulithi, we had a list, but it didn't seem as great as we had when we had the actual collision.

Q: You went back in company with a couple of carriers, the Cabot and the Hancock. Any recollections of that trip to Pearl Harbor?

Mr. Bak: It was a happy feeling, with great anticipation, knowing we were going back home, knowing that we wouldn't be involved in any action, knowing that we were still alive, and knowing that we were looking forward to our liberty. It was just a happy feeling, knowing that we were leaving the war zone and not having to worry about going to general quarters. In fact, I don't remember one general quarters sounding the entire time of going back to Pearl Harbor. We continued the same four and eight watch and that also gave us an opportunity to rest. So it was just a routine kind of a thing. Even though we were leaving the war zone, we still couldn't put lights on at night, no running lights, no smoking aboard topside. We had to be careful in closing the hatches to make sure there was no light appearing.

Q: You mentioned before that you noticed some differences in Honolulu this time from what you'd seen previously. It seemed to be more subdued on the beach.

Mr. Bak: The first time we were there, we were all preparing for the big push, a lot of ships coming in, a lot of ships going out. I believe at the time we came back, we didn't seem to have that tightness of security in Honolulu. Although I believe they still had curfew in Honolulu, it wasn't as restrictive as it was during the early part of the war.

Q: Did your crew feel a sense of relief to get out of the war zone?

Mr. Bak: Oh, yes, everybody was very happy. The conversation aboard ship was very pleasant. When you'd go in to breakfast and lunch and dinner, you knew you were going home. It was a bubbly kind of enthusiasm, I think, going back, because everyone was alive, everyone was going back, and we had a lot of stories to tell, we felt. Although when I got home later on, after the war was over, nobody would listen to your stories, so I kept them to myself until you came along.

Although we had some screening to do with those two carriers during our trip, we never worried about enemy aircraft or enemy ships. We did not have one submarine scare on the way back from Ulithi to Honolulu.

Q: Now you got a new commanding officer in Hawaii,

Lieutenant Commander E.B. Henry. What are your recollections of him?

Mr. Bak: Henry was a slight fellow, very quiet, it seemed to me, very serious. And it just seemed like he was completely different from the other two captains we had. Maybe because I felt that he wasn't with us during the time of battle, I didn't have that closeness with him. Even though I was on the bridge with him, we didn't have that day-to-day routine of battle stations. In other words, I never had Captain Henry come out to the bridge and yell, "Bak, what are the battle lights?"--you know, just keep you on your toes constantly and make sure everything was done right aboard ship. So it was just an easy routine from a captain who picked up a ship that was going back home State-side, and it was a different feeling entirely. It was just like the war was over almost for us, going home on leave and liberty.

Q: Well, according to the ship's history, the voyage took a week. He came on board the 22nd of April, and you got to Bremerton, Washington, on the 29th.

Mr. Bak: Right after that, I had a 30-day leave starting from May first. We had a split leave period, if I recall. They had two groups going. I was in the first group. That's why I didn't know Henry that well. It just seemed that he was efficient, he knew his stuff. But the crew being together so long and then getting a new captain, after everything happened, going back was a different feeling. I think the crew didn't know Henry too well either, though he might have been a great guy. Had he been with us in battle at sea, we would have thought the world of the guy. The officers were very happy with Henry.

Q: That's interesting--that it's almost as if he had to prove himself to the crew.

Mr. Bak: That's what I thought of him, you know.

It reminded me, when I was aboard ship for the first time and I met all the fellows who were to sea before, and they may have had hash marks, they may have had battle stars. They ignored us completely, because we were just rookies. Later on, when I was at sea and we earned some battle stars and we came back in, and we got new crew members aboard, we looked at those new members and thought, "Gee, they're rookies." So I think it was the same feeling. You had to prove yourself, and then once you were part of the team, and you're under fire, you felt pretty good about yourself. And you couldn't wait to put your battle stars on and get your ribbons on and walk down the street, hoping somebody would notice them. It was a salty thing to do.

Q: Did you go back to New Jersey on your leave?

Mr. Bak: Yes. In fact, I called Anne on the phone from Seattle, Washington.* I knew Anne before the war and told her I was coming home, and she was surprised to hear from me, because I maybe wrote her one letter during the entire war. I was not a good letter writer to females because of the fact that I didn't want to be involved in anything; I just wanted to do my duty. I went back to New Jersey. They arranged a flight for me from Seattle to New York. If I recall, it made about 13 stops along the way. It was a DC-3. It was a very long time getting back home. Then we had a 30-day leave. And that's when my 30-day leave started back home, and my brother Andy, who just passed away on Saturday morning, was home on leave from the Marine Corps.** He was a Marine down in Norfolk and never left for overseas duty. He was home on leave, and a bunch of other fellows were home on leave at the same time that I was.

The family had a big sign on our house saying, "Welcome home, Mike." When I called them on the phone to say I was coming home, they were very happy to hear about that, and they made all kinds of preparations to have a party. All our friends knew I was coming home, so it was kind of a neat thing, a nice homecoming feeling.

I lived two doors from the local gin mill, where

---
*Anne Gudzon, Passaic, New Jersey--now Mrs. Bak.
**Corporal Andrew Bak, USMC.

everybody hung out, and it was right across the street from the fire department, where I was involved before the war as a volunteer. I went back home and met a lot of friends, had a lot of parties, tried to look up old girlfriends, and I visited with Anne. Anne, at that time, was in the hospital for an appendectomy. So I came in the hospital with some flowers and she was kind of shocked.

So that was the first time Anne and I went together, and we had a lot of fun--a lot of visits with my friends. And I also had a sad moment. I found out a friend of mine, Wally Maciag, was killed in action in Europe while serving in the Army. He lived a block away, and he was one of my close friends in boyhood days. So I went over to see his father, whom I knew very well. When I got there, his father never said "Boo." I tried to carry on a conversation, and the father wouldn't talk at all; he was just depressed about his son being killed. I was amazed, because I knew the man real well. Yet here I was. I guess maybe he wondered why his son died and why not me. After a short period of time, I left the home feeling kind of depressed, because I wanted to offer my condolences, and I just felt that he didn't accept them, for whatever reason. That was the last time I ever saw the man.

Then we had some friends of ours that we used to correspond with who had parties for us. It was just a neat time. At the time I was home, another very important thing happened--VE Day.* I remember it very distinctly. A couple of us, myself and two other sailors who were home on leave, went to Manhattan and were in Times Square on VE Day, which was tremendous. It was a great feeling; everybody was very happy, everybody was kissing each other--just a nice feeling. It was a time of your life when you went to a local bar to have a beer, and you met a lot of other sailors, a lot of other soldiers, a lot of Marines and a lot of Coast Guard people.

Yet the strange thing about it, when I went back home, I thought I was in a lot of action, did a lot of things, and I thought people would be interested in hearing about them. But nobody seemed to care. It was just the feeling, I guess, like the Vietnam soldiers who came back home, nobody cared. They cared in the sense that I was home, but what happened out there was just history. So, as a result, I rarely ever talked about what we did. If I mentioned that we were in a storm or we collided with the battleship New Jersey, it seemed to go in one ear and out the other ear. That we shot down six Jap planes and sank a submarine didn't mean anything, because everybody else was in action. They didn't want to talk about it; they just wanted to have a good time and forget about it. I guess they thought about civilian life more than anything else. It's like hitting a home run in the ball park and nobody cheered.

---
*VE Day, 8 May 1945, marked the victory of the Allies in Europe.

Q: How were you treated by civilians in general?

Mr. Bak: Everyone was just as friendly as could be. Every house seemed to have either a blue star in the window, representing a family member in service, or a gold star hung in the window if a member of the family was killed. Whenever they would see you, they just felt very happy that you were home. They would tell you their son was overseas somewhere else, and they received letters from him. We exchanged information about where they were, where we were, and so forth, that if they write to them, "Give them our best love and regards." It was a very happy time. People were very friendly, because everyone seemed to have somebody in the military. It's amazing how the current generation has no idea of what the feeling was back then. They never will, because I don't think a war like that will ever happen again.

Q: I hope not.

Mr. Bak: I hope not, too. So I think the current generation will never know that feeling of complete cohesiveness of one effort--the "win the war, beat the Japs" kind of a feeling. It was a neat thing. As a result, everybody invited you to their home for dinner, for a party. So they were just pleased and happy to you were back home, hoped you'd be home again soon when the war was over.

Q: I would guess that those 30 days passed very quickly.

Mr. Bak: Too quickly! We had one incident. My brother Andy was a member of the volunteer fire department, because he was 21 at the time. We had a Coast Guard man who also was a member of the fire department and was over 21, and another sailor who was over 21, and myself, sitting in the gin mill right two doors from my home, right across the street from the fire department. A hook and ladder truck was housed in the fire department, and after we had a few beers, somebody said, "Let's take the fire truck out for a ride."

I said, "Look, I know a few girls from high school days. We'll stop by and see if they want to go for a ride on the fire truck."

The four of us took the truck out of the fire department without permission. I didn't steer. My brother handled the tiller. Another fellow named Bennie Perrini drove the front part of the truck, in military uniforms, and whenever we passed a girl's home that I knew, we'd blow the siren. If they came out, we'd ask them to go for a ride, but they were afraid, you know; geez, they were all afraid.

So to make a long story short, we rode the truck, I would say, for at least an hour. At my brother's funeral on Saturday--I should say on Monday night at the wake--I ran into the captain of the fire department, a fellow by the name of Hector Savioli. I mention this incident because I said, "Hey, Hector, do you remember the time the fire truck was taken out?"

He said, "Yes. You know what happened? It was Sunday afternoon, and I came into the fire department, opened the door, and the truck was gone. I knew there was no fire." He couldn't imagine what in the hell happened to the truck.

Then we brought the truck back without any accident, fortunately. We weren't drunk, but just feeling good. Then we parked the truck in a V-shape, right smack at the corner of the fire department, and we all took photographs of the truck, in uniform standing there. We blocked all the traffic, and then we parked the truck in the building.

The next day, each of us left for his respective military base. After the war was over, I joined the fire department. A court of inquiry was held to find out who was responsible. The city council fathers were very upset about the incident of the sailors and the Marine responsible for taking the truck out illegally. We had to testify to what happened. They let us go after a strong reprimand. But that was an incident that happened when we were at home on leave.

Q: Was it tough then, having to make the return trip out to Bremerton again?

Mr. Bak: It was kind of exciting, because I was anxious to return and visit with the crew, because after living with the crew for two and a half years, you sort of missed them. They were very close; they were closer than any of my friends back home because of what we went through.

Q: You had a close bond, because you'd been through some life-threatening experiences.

Mr. Bak: Yea, we had a very close bond, and I was anxious to get back. It was kind of sad in one way to leave home, but then you were anxious because you knew you were going to have the ship repaired. You knew you were going to the war zone again. You knew you were going to go out and be part of the action, be part of the scene. When we got back to Seattle, the other members of the crew went home for 30 days' leave. The fellows who returned to the ship in Seattle had a lot of fun. We went out together in the evening, and it was just a pleasant party time.

Q: Did you go in the town of Bremerton itself?

Mr. Bak: I didn't remember Bremerton too well. Bremerton never appealed to me--for some reason or other, I have very few recollections of Bremerton, even though we were there a long time. I always liked Seattle. I always liked the ferryboat ride on the Kalakala. Seattle was a much bigger city. I don't know, Bremerton seemed like it was just full of sailors constantly. And if you wanted to meet somebody--a young lady or something--it would not be the place in Bremerton, because the place was loaded with sailors. Seattle offered more opportunities for meeting someone or having fun.

We went out in a group constantly to a place where there might be dancing and hopefully might find some young lady to dance with and perhaps make a date. At this point, having all your battle ribbons on, you felt a lot different from the first time you were in Seattle. Back then nobody would pay attention to us because they knew we were recruits. They could tell by the uniform I had the rating of a first class petty officer.

Q: What do you recall about the repairs? Were there any items of modernization done during that time?

Mr. Bak: There were always a lot of electrical lines over the side, fellows with blow torches, and you could see a lot of repairs made to the superstructure. But I didn't pay too much attention to what was being done to the ship. It just seemed there were a lot of workmen aboard the ship who were doing things and repairing the ship where we had the damage. I believe a lot of that repair work was completed in the first month of my leave back home. I was gone about four weeks. When I got back, we could see already there was a lot of rewelding, putting plates back up, and getting the ship back ready. They were supposed to have the ship ready in two months, and they were ready in two months. I don't remember too much of what they actually did. I knew they were repairing, a lot of workmen were on, and every time you got up in the morning around 8:00 o'clock, they would be over there loading their stuff on. You always had to sort of walk over lines or walk around different things, acetylene tanks that were used for welding.

Q: It was probably very noisy also.

Mr. Bak: It was very noisy, very noisy a lot of hubbub.

Q: Then it came time, after the second group got back, to have some training and shakedown before the cruise west.

Mr. Bak: Yes, we had another shakedown. It just seemed like we were a brand-new ship going on a shakedown cruise for the first time. Because of the accident, they wanted to make sure structurally the ship was sound. We had a lot of firing of the guns in the shakedown cruise and did a lot of maneuvering and a lot of testing of the equipment, similar to the testing we did the first time around.

Q: Had there been much turnover in the crew?

Mr. Bak: Yes, there was a lot of turnover in the crew. In fact, when I got back, it seemed that a lot of fellows were transferred off the ship for new assignments, and we missed quite a few crew members. If you asked for somebody, you might hear, "Oh, he's already been transferred somewhere else." And all of a sudden they disappeared. Then you'd make new friends. But most of the fellows I palled around with all came back to the ship. I would say that almost every guy that I palled around with came back on the second cruise out of Seattle.

Q: Then it came time for you to head west toward Eniwetok. Did the crew have more of a regard for Captain Henry by this time, would you say?

Mr. Bak: Yea, we got to know him a little better. We all liked Henry. He seemed like a competent officer, but he seemed very quiet. I don't remember him raising his voice like Captain Stephan--boy, you'd know he was around. Captain Henry was a reserved guy. He had his binoculars on always, looking around. He'd come in, stick his head in to the bridge and "Right full rudder." He didn't have that authoritative voice that I was used to in the command. I would say that even Lidstone had a greater authoritative voice than Henry did.

Q: During that time, you found out that the hostilities were over. What was the reaction in your ship?

Mr. Bak: The reaction was one of, I guess, euphoria, because we all felt we did our job, and we felt that we'd be going back home some day, and that we beat the Japs. It was just a happy feeling of camaraderie. I think one of the greatest things that happened at the time when they announced that we'd won the war was the fact that we were able to put the running lights on aboard ship and be able to walk the decks with lights on. It was just a very strange, eerie feeling--it's no longer dark! You don't have to bump your feet into a hatch somewhere or feel your way around like we did in very dark nights. So it was a very happy feeling.

I think the biggest thing we all felt was that we were alive, we didn't get hit, and we didn't get killed. We would be going home, safe and sound.

It was a long war; it had been a war where we'd seen a lot of things happen. And some of the memories that stick with you of the dead bodies floating in the water, all bloated up, that you'd seen during the invasion of some of these islands. It was kind of a feeling that, Jesus, it could be you, for that matter.

Q: This was also the time when the first two atomic bombs

were dropped. What was the discussion on your ship about that?

Mr. Bak: Looking back, in August 1945 we were in Pearl Harbor awaiting reassignment to the fleet. We finished our shakedown cruise of the Franks after repairs were made. On August the sixth, we heard the first announcement that Hiroshima was hit by an atom bomb. I never knew what an atom bomb was; I never heard of an atom bomb. But I understood from the accounts that we heard by newspaper, radio, and ship's information that it was the most awesome bomb ever made, and that it killed many, many people in Hiroshima. The first feeling we had, we were not too happy for the Japanese, but we felt very, very happy about the fact that the bomb was dropped and that we were doing a number of Japan. Even though so many people were killed, we felt good about it. I felt good about it, because I thought it was a way of ending the war sooner, and maybe not getting killed myself. But it was an awesome feeling. At that point, everybody heard about an atom bomb; they were talking about it and talking about the destructive power of the bomb and what it was doing, and hoped that it could end the war soon. It was an awesome feeling to know that we had a bomb of that magnitude and that we had people capable of producing such a bomb.

Then a few days later, we had the announcement that on August the ninth--we were under way to the Marshall Islands at the time from Pearl Harbor when the announcement was made that Nagasaki was hit by an atom bomb. And the same day that we dropped the bomb, Russia declared war on Japan. Separately, we heard announcements from our ship's radio that Task Force 38 carrier planes were making devastating strikes against northern Honshu. So these were some of the things that were happening as we were going out to the war zone. These events seemed to make it clearer and clearer that the war might be over pretty soon, and it was a good feeling that our country was doing these things. Maybe not a good feeling for the people who were killed, but we all felt it had to be done, and that President Truman made the right decision by dropping that bomb. Because there was some talk about the invasion of the mainland could be a long, tedious job during the war, and it could have meant many, many, many thousands of Americans being killed.

Q: You didn't stay long in the Marshalls; you went on over to Japan itself. What are your recollections there?

Mr. Bak: When we went over toward Japan, we joined Task Force 38 again, and we were screening the task force carriers to prevent any strikes or any maybe suicidal missions from the Japanese planes who might have taken off from Japan after Japan announced the surrender. I believe the surrender was announced August the 15th. On August 15th, at around 12:00 noon, according to my notes, Halsey notified Task Force 38 that orders had been received from commander in chief of the Navy to stop all offensive operations against Japan. In fact, when I was at our reunion last year in October, in San Diego, one of the officers, the radio officer, had the original copies that we received by radio announcing the war was over. I made photocopies of both announcements, so that's why I know exactly what was said when the war ended.

On August 14th, an aircraft carrier launched strikes over Tokyo, and at 6:30, Admiral Halsey, aboard the USS Missouri, had notified Task Force 38 he had received an urgent message from Commander in Chief Pacific ordering all air operations to cease. "The Jap Emperor has promised to surrender." That was on the 14th. On the 15th, he actually did surrender.

On the 16th, the first troops started to arrive, I believe, in Japan. On August the 23rd, we arrived outside of Sagami Wan with the aircraft carriers to maintain surveillance over Tokyo and eastern Honshu. The major units of the Third Fleet entered Sagami Wan and anchored in selected berths. On August 27th, the minesweepers started to sweep the entrance to Tokyo Bay.

Q: Where was your ship at the time of the surrender ceremony aboard the Missouri on September second?

Mr. Bak: On September the first, we were part of Destroyer Division 94 and Squadron 47 with the Fifth Fleet, and Admiral Spruance in the USS New Jersey was in charge.* We reported for duty with Commander Task Group 38.4 under Rear Admiral Bogan.** We were with Carrier Division Four; he was in the USS Randolph. On September fourth and fifth, we were reassigned to Task Group 38.1 with Carrier Division Six, which was part of the Yorktown group. On September first, we were cruising off the southeastern coast of Japan with Task Unit 30.8, Commander Escort Division 49, USS Reynolds, a DE, which was screening the task unit. We were just off of the southeast coast of Japan at that time, and we were acting as a plane guard ship for the USS Gilbert Islands (CVE-107).

On September the second, the date of the surrender, we were assigned to Task Unit 30.7.42. We were in rendezvous on the southeastern coast of Honshu in accordance with a secret dispatch. We just were maneuvering back and forth with the carriers to make sure no enemy aircraft was approaching or trying to do any damage to our forces. We were just outside of Tokyo. There was a feeling that there might be some suicide Japanese planes in the sky. I remember the instructions came over very vividly and clearly. Our leaders told the Japanese government that if any airplane appeared in the sky, Allied forces had been

---

*Admiral Raymond A. Spruance, USN, Commander Fifth Fleet.
**Rear Admiral Gerald F. Bogan, USN, whose oral history is in the Naval Institute collection.

given instructions to shoot immediately. So our function was to be ready for a surprise suicide attack.

Q: In this time just after the end of the war, was there a relaxation as far as discipline? Did you have more opportunities for recreation?

Mr. Bak: There was not a hell of a lot we could do on board ship.

Q: What are your memories of going ashore in Japan?

Mr. Bak: The first memory I have was that we tied up at the Japanese naval base at Yokosuka. We tied up, and then we had to walk down this long pier toward the naval base. There were a bunch of young Japanese kids, boys and girls, maybe 8, 9, 10, 11 years old, looking for handouts, putting their hands out. They couldn't talk in English, just looking for something that we would give them. Then a short distance behind them, maybe 50-100 yards away, were the parents of these kids. We would walk down. None of us who were going on liberty had any guns on them, because they were not allowed to carry guns in peacetime.

I went with a fellow crew member by the name of Gene Reardon.* A professional wrestler, he was known as "Gentleman Gene." He was from Kansas City. In fact, I

---
*Eugene Reardon.

bumped into him at the reunion that we had in San Diego. He and I left the naval base, and we walked around the area of Yokosuka, not knowing where to go or what to do. We saw an Army truck come by, and we hitched a ride. They were going to west Tokyo, so we jumped in and sat on the back of the Army flatbed truck that was covered with a tarpaulin, had no sides to it, and under the tarpaulin we found out later it was black market goods that they were taking somewhere to west Tokyo to sell. We sat on this truck and got a ride all the way in. For a while we saw nobody but Japanese people. We spent several hours with the Army guys; they took us around and gave us a nice tour. Then they stopped in West Tokyo, and they started selling black market goods to the Japanese

Q: Such as what?

Mr. Bak: Mostly foodstuffs. They would get yen in the exchange. We were helping them sell, because we were so appreciative of the ride.

Then when it came time to go back, they gave us instructions how to get back by train. There was a train going back from Tokyo to Yokohama to Yokosuka.

While we roamed around west Tokyo and Tokyo, there were periods of time we saw nobody but Japanese people. There was just two of us. We kind of looked back later on and said, "Hey, we were kind of stupid to be there by ourselves and roaming around." The only conversation I had with any Japanese, I met some fellow who came up to me, a Japanese fellow, who spoke very good English, an elderly gentleman. He said, "Hello. How are you?"

I said, "Fine. How are you?" We sat down and we talked. We talked about five or ten minutes, just shot the breeze about the war and glad it was over; he was glad it was over. He seemed to want to talk about how happy he was that nobody was going to get hurt anymore. Just had a nice visit with him. Then we headed back towards the area of Yokohama.

I had liberty several times in Japan. The first time we went there, we stayed around Yokosuka and Yokohama. Then I went to Tokyo. The biggest thing I remember--I wrote an article that appeared in the hometown paper later on--was the fact that it was just desolate, and bombed out. We saw nothing but ruins, and how people lived in that ruin is beyond me. Why didn't they end the war a lot sooner? Because all the buildings seemed to be down, and a lot of people were scavenging through the ruins to pick up whatever they could, whether it was tin for new homes or whatever. A lot of poverty. It was kind of a neat thing to visit a foreign land, but, on the other hand, it was just depressing to see what the ruins were as a result of the war.

We brought our own food. I bought a Japanese beer. I brought some money with me. In fact, they gave us some

Japanese money. At that time--I don't know why I remember this--but it was 15 yen to an American dollar in 1945. This sticks in my mind. We were given Japanese money in exchange for American money. We thought we'd buy souvenirs, look around for anything we could pick up as souvenirs. But we were afraid to touch anything because it might be poisoned. We did see some Imperial Japanese cars come by occasionally, with a flag with stars on it, signifying that they may have been some high-ranking Japanese officers. As they came by, they saluted and we saluted as the car came by. So it was just a matter of walking around an area and hitchhiking.

After we were in west Tokyo, we got back on a train that the GIs told us about, because we could speak no Japanese and we could find nobody speaking English. I'd never seen a train so jammed in my life before. They were hanging on the sides and all over. We were told to get off at a certain stop and we did. So we got back to the ship.

Another time I went over, we got caught in a typhoon. A typhoon came up when our ship was at anchor in the bay somewhere, and we couldn't get back to our ship. I was stranded and put on another big cargo ship for about a day until the typhoon subsided, and they put me on a whaleboat and sent me back to our ship.

I remember close by to the area we were at, there must have been a lot of Japanese geisha houses or whorehouses, whatever they called them, because at this point the Army was in Japan, and we could see their Army shoes in certain houses. And they would say that would be a Japanese whorehouse. We stayed away from them, because we were just scared shitless to do anything as far as going anywhere out of bounds. But somehow the GIs seemed to find these places.

But that is my recollection of Japan. We didn't want to eat anything. We took our own canteen of water and some cheese sandwiches that the cook would prepare for us. We tried to pick up some souvenirs. I did manage to visit a factory of some kind that was bombed out. We picked up some tools. I got some nice tools that I took with me and brought back to the ship. I thought I did a good thing to take them back home with me, but somebody aboard ship swiped them from me and I didn't get them back. I don't know who it was. They were goners.

At this point in time aboard ship, we had to be very careful of things disappearing and missing, because as we were getting closer to home, you might find things missing.

Q: This is a contrast to what you had mentioned before.

Mr. Bak: It was a contrast to what I mentioned before, yes, because I think there was a lot of souvenir hunting going on in Japan. I think now that the war was over and we were going back--I know I was disappointed. I thought I had a good thing going and some nice tools, but they were gone. I had no idea who took them.

In fact, when we got back Stateside, when we left the ship eventually, we had to take our sea bags and empty them out on the dock completely to make sure that nothing was in a sea bag that belonged to the United States Navy.

Q: How would you describe the demeanor of the Japanese people toward American sailors in uniform?

Mr. Bak: They were polite, and every time we walked down the street, they would just keep to one side of us and point. I just remember vividly them pointing at probably my rating of three stripes. Nobody made any threat to us; nobody made any kind of a remark. They just seemed to go about their business as usual, except that if we walked down the street on the sidewalk with a lot of Japs, they would just open up and let us go by. I remember Gene, one time--he was a big fellow, a very strapping guy--picked up two small Japs and held them up by their clothes, you know; they were kicking their feet. Then he put them down, smiling. He was a big, likable guy, smiling. We just kept waving at everybody and smiling and trying to be as friendly as we possibly could, to give them the feeling that we weren't there to hurt them, and hopefully they wouldn't hurt us.

We did some stupid things when we were in Japan. We were going to places we probably shouldn't have been. We

Bak #3 - 229

were looking for souvenirs, anything that we could take back with us, and not having any wheels other than the ride from the GIs. We would go looking for places that possibly would have something. I don't know what we were looking for. We were looking for something we might take back home that was good. So we were in places we shouldn't have been probably.

Q: Were there any official directives on how to conduct yourself ashore?

Mr. Bak: Yes. We didn't want to antagonize the Japs, we didn't want to treat them unfairly and unjustly. Make sure that you have your behavior in line with your behavior back home, not to offend the Japanese people in any way. I did have a Jap beer; I remember tasting a Jap beer.

Q: How as it?

Mr. Bak: It was good. Looking back, it was a nice, warm day. It wasn't too cold, and it was just pleasant. At that time of September, it was a good time of the year.

Q: What were your official duties at this point? What was the ship supposed to be doing?

Mr. Bak: I would say mainly rest and recreation for the

crew. They gave us liberty based upon, I guess, port and starboard liberty.

Q: Did you have any training at all during this period?

Mr. Bak: Not to my knowledge, no. I don't remember any training at all.

Q: When did you start losing crew members through the demobilization?

Mr. Bak: We lost some in Tokyo Bay. Most of the crew members were being lost when we got to the United States. We got into Astoria, Oregon, on Navy Day, the 27th of October. We pulled in with a cruiser named <u>Pittsburgh</u>. I think each ship in the Navy was assigned to a certain specific port. I guess Navy Day was the day they were supposed to arrive. So we arrived in Astoria, Oregon. We were there for Navy Day. We arrived maybe the day before Navy Day. I remember we pulled in to the pier; there was a band out there, a lot of Red Cross people, doughnuts, coffee and milk on a stand. We got off the ship, and we started having liberty in Astoria shortly after our arrival. I think we came in probably on a Friday, because we were transported a day or two later by bus to a football game either in Eugene--it was either a University of Oregon or an Oregon State football game. It was a Saturday, about a good couple of hours ride by bus from Astoria to wherever the game was at. We were the guests of honor at this football game, and they announced during the time that we had members of the USS _Franks_ and the cruiser _Pittsburgh_ for Navy Day. The ship was shipshape, looking good. The men were all dressed in their uniforms, clean and neat as a whistle.

Q: Had you come in with a homeward bound pennant?

Mr. Bak: No. I don't remember the homeward bound pennant on our ship at all. We should have had one on, but for some reason, I don't remember that.

Q: Then the loss of crew members did set in, I would guess. How did that affect the ship?

Mr. Bak: In November we arrived in the San Pedro area. I remember there were a lot of meetings with Navy personnel who gave us instructions about what we could expect in civilian life, who gave us information about our insurance, gave us information about possible schooling, education, and asking us if we wanted to ship over. At that time I was quartermaster first, and an officer wanted to know if I wanted to reenlist in the Navy. They gave you a pitch. They didn't push you; they just gave you all of the options and you made up your own decision. In fact, one of the officers said I could make chief in a short time if I'd reenlist. But I was anxious to get out.

As far as the other crew members, since we were in port in November, we were getting quite a bit of liberty. So some of our guys started leaving the ship. I was one of the first guys to leave. I left January the tenth. So between November and January, we had a lot of liberty in and around the Los Angeles area. In fact, I remember I went to the Rose Bowl parade on January the first, 1946, and tried to go to the Rose Bowl game between USC and Alabama, but the tickets were sold out. But I did watch the parade. I had friends living in Santa Monica; in fact, a crew member was from Santa Monica--Charlie Lewis. I visited with his folks and stayed overnight, and from there we went to the parade on January the first.

At that time, each crew member had a certain amount of points built up, based upon his war record. Based on that number is when you were going to be discharged. Since I was one of the first ones aboard ship, I was off the ship a lot sooner than most members. As far as the other fellows are concerned, I guess they disappeared one at a time. I remember Bill Middleton stayed in the Navy for a while, but he left before that; he was gone before that.* He went to submarine duty. But as far as the rest of the fellows, we sort of drifted apart.

---

*Quartermaster Second Class William Middleton.

Q: Was that sort of a dull period?

Mr. Bak: It was a dull period. It was a period of time that we had to put in. A lot of recreation, a lot of visiting, a lot of liberty.

Q: What were some of the other liberty attractions there in the San Pedro area?

Mr. Bak: I would say the biggest attraction was the Palladium Dance Palace in Los Angeles, where a number of the guys would always seem to wind up. But the problem we had, being in San Pedro, was the distance to Los Angeles. If you met some young lady that you wanted to maybe date, she might live on the other side of the San Fernando Valley. So you were visiting Hollywood, visiting museums in the area itself, going to the movies, maybe trying to meet some young ladies, which was very difficult.

Q: Why?

Mr. Bak: It was just a matter of logistics. There were so many sailors around constantly, so many servicemen, number one. Then, too, you had no wheels to get around. Taxi rides were expensive. I think maybe I had one or two dates in the Los Angeles area, which was not a hell of a lot. Then, again, we were just roaming around, sight-seeing. We went around in groups or in pairs, constantly, just visiting different places. So the social activity was very limited. I didn't know anybody out there other than Charlie Lewis, whose aunt and uncle lived in Santa Monica. So it was a difficult kind of a time to meet anybody. At that time, the war was over, and all the ships were coming back in, and there were sailors all over the place, holy Christ, everywhere you went. I guess maybe the ladies in the area were either vouched for or were afraid of sailors. The war was over, and the mothers kept all the daughters in.

The biggest area where there seemed to be young ladies would be at the dance places. Wherever there was an American Legion dance or a dance at the Palladium or some service club or some church organization, that's where we would go. They would provide refreshments.

Q: Were you impatient to get out of the Navy at that point?

Mr. Bak: Yes, I was very impatient. I was looking forward to seeing my relatives and friends of mine who were in the service.

We were happy to get out. In fact, my mother had all my paraphernalia--all my clothes, all my records, all my medals and stuff in the house where we lived, up in the attic, and she warned me, "Get it out of there." So Anne and I got married in July of '47, and then we moved out of the home and got our own apartment. My mother kept warning me, "Get it out. Get it out," for about four or five years, and then finally she threw everything out.

I was happy to get out of the Navy. I thoroughly enjoyed it, but once it was all over, I got right back in the civilian routine, going from one side of the fence, where my whole life previously was centered around how many hits I received playing baseball for a semi-pro team, you know, maybe an occasional date, working and trying to scrape up enough money for an automobile, and then I joined the Navy. Then all of a sudden, on the other side of the fence you're out of the Navy and starting your civilian life again. It was kind of a period of time that I was happy to get out of the Navy. We were just tickled pink to get out. The war was over. I guess you wanted to get back home to your family and back home to your friends.

Q: Did you have some firm goals in mind at that point?

Mr. Bak: At that point, no. I should have had better goals than I finally had. I stayed home for a couple of months, got bored, then went back to work where I was previously employed. Then I went back to college in September.

Q: Where did you go to college?

Mr. Bak: I went to Paterson State Teachers College in Paterson, New Jersey, located about 7 miles from Garfield. I didn't sleep away at college. I was on the GI Bill of rights. While I was there, I played varsity basketball and baseball for the college teams. So that's when civilian life became fun again.

Then that year Anne and I were steadily dating, and we finally got married in July of '47. In that time of my life, which was almost 39 years ago, I had 38 months of eligibility remaining on my GI Bill of Rights. It was then I decided to get involved in industry. I read an article about a department store chain called Allied Stores, which was originating a new retail marketing program called executive training program on the GI Bill of Rights. It was a program of half a day training in school on the GI Bill of Rights in this department store chain and became a buyer of greeting cards, typewriters, stationery, and candy. After about two years, I graduated from this program. I was in the first training program of the Allied Stores Corporation in a department store in North Jersey. Allied today is the biggest department store chain in the United States and probably the world.

So that's what happened. I left school, got married, and joined the department store business. That's how I got involved with the company I am with today. I used to buy an awful lot of typewriters for the department store, advertising and promoting them in the newspaper, and the company that I bought machines from offered me a job to do the selling for them, because they were so impressed with the job that we did and the amount of machines that we sold and promoted through the store, that they offered me a job to sell their equipment. The job was attractive from the standpoint that they offered me an automobile and expenses, five days a week, no Saturday work, and no Thursday nights til 9:00. So I was playing golf every Saturday, and it was kind of neat. It was a lot more money than I was making. I was married and raising a family. So I've been with the company ever since; I've been there around 36 years.

Q: This is Olivetti?

Mr. Bak: It was Underwood in those days. Underwood was purchased by Olivetti in 1959, so I was with Underwood for a period of about nine years before Olivetti took over, and that's where I'm at today--Olivetti USA as a national account executive.

Q: Any overall thoughts to wrap up your naval experience?

Mr. Bak: From the standpoint of a young, impressionable fellow, I thoroughly enjoyed it. It gave me an opportunity to see the world and be part of the greatest armada in the history of naval warfare, and being part of a winning team, participating in things that very few people will ever get a chance to see or ever see again. I was impressed with the professionalism of the United States Navy and the tremendous amount of training that our ship was involved in. It was a very first-class operation, I thought. Looking back now, it was a very costly thing. I guess it still is today.

Q: That's the price you pay to preserve your society.

Mr. Bak: That's right. So I was tickled pink to be part of an organization that I always wanted to join when I was a young boy but never thought I could because it was such a difficult program to get into. But once I was into the program itself, I thoroughly enjoyed it.

I think one of the greatest things that happened to me was the fact that I became a quartermaster in the Navy. Not knowing what a quartermaster was when I joined the Navy and then realizing, after I was aboard ship, that I had a rating that was a very nice rating from the standpoint that you were constantly aware of what was happening because your duties were on the bridge, and because of this, I think I had a better feel for what was happening on the ship than most of the fellows on our ship.

Q: I wonder if you had somewhat mixed feelings upon leaving the Franks. On the one hand, you were eager to get on with your life in the postwar world, but you were leaving these people that you'd been associated with for so long.

Mr. Bak: That was a mixed feeling I had. It was difficult. It was very difficult. For a period of time, we corresponded with each other, and then all of a sudden things stopped completely. I think we all got married probably eventually, all had the problems of raising a family and trying to earn a living, so we lost track of each other. But you're right, it was a period of time, and we can even look back right now, a lot of memories return and you hope you can see some of the guys again. When the reunions come up, why, it's a great feeling to review some of the things we accomplished, and the camaraderie. I think the camaraderie today is great in the reunion group, because we reminisce on the things we did. But it was a tough feeling, leaving the Navy. I was just happy to get out. I was not what you'd call a guy that wanted to be in the Navy as his career.

Q: Were there any values and experiences from that Navy time that stuck with you, that had an effect on your later life?

Mr. Bak: Well, I guess the values of the professionalism. I was so impressed with the officers on board the ship, who were very professional, very well trained, very well educated. I guess the value of camaraderie, pulling together, one effort, being part of a winning team.

As far as the effect it had on me, I was just proud to have been part of the United States Navy. One of the greatest thrills is to look back and say, "Hey, I was there when the greatest battles were fought." They will probably go down in history as the greatest battles. Being in a typhoon and surviving a typhoon that lost three ships and lost a lot of men, and being in battles, being right there where the action was, I think was a great thrill. Young fellows today don't have that thrill. It's just part of a life that I'm glad it happened the way it happened. I'm glad I was there in the age I was then.

Q: Have you ever speculated on what direction your life might have taken had there not been a war then and not the opportunity to serve in the Navy?

Mr. Bak: I don't think my life, if there was no war, would have been as exciting as it has been, because it opened up to me areas of adventure that I never would have had. For example, here I was as a young boy in Honolulu on Waikiki Beach. To this day, some friends of mine have never been to Honolulu. I say, "I was there when I was 20 years old." It just seems like you're bragging, but I was there. All these things open up to you. I think a world of travel, a world of being part of a service organization really has a very good effect on anybody.

I think, personally, every young man should be part of the military and should be part of the United States Government--there should be rules or regulations or government laws to make everyone at least take part in two or three years of service, in any service in the United States forces. Because without that, you don't have the opportunities of meeting different kinds of people, get a chance to know regimentation, get a chance to get wholesome instructions, give instructions. For example, right now I don't think young kids today ever have the feeling of doing an oblique march in the Navy or marching together as a group. They laugh at it today, but that feeling of walking down the street to chow with a bunch of guys, singing a song, right face, left face, you know.

When I visit military bases now on business, I look back and I watch some of these happenings, I feel a little nostalgia. For example, we were in San Diego. We were invited by the San Diego Naval Training Station to witness the graduation ceremony of the boot camp, and we were in the stands with thousands of people watching this boot camp ceremony for graduation of several different companies. Each company had a flag-raising, and the bugle blowing, they're marching along and the band was playing. That's when it really hit home, I guess, missing the Navy, of seeing all of that pomp and circumstance and watching these kids graduate, seeing young kids coming past you. Those guys are wearing the same uniform that I wore, knowing they're going on to different locations and ships, and so forth, at sea, but knowing, still, they won't have the same experiences I had because it was wartime. From that standpoint, I think it was a great, great thrill to be part of a war effort that was very successful.

Q: You are a representative of the millions of people of your generation who had that sort of experience, but I would think that not a lot of it has been recorded. So I'm very grateful to you for taking this time to preserve these memories through the medium of oral history, and leave them as a record for years to come.

Mr. Bak: I certainly want to thank you for the opportunity to do this, because I enjoyed it. A lot of memories came back.

Appendices

to

Reminiscences of

Mr. Michael Bak, Jr.

## Retrievers Of Ditched Pilots
### By ERNIE PYLE

IN THE WESTERN PACIFIC—Destroyers love to pick up airplane pilots out of the ocean. When they rescued our Lt. Jimmy Van Fleet, of Findlay, Ohio, after his plane had plunged over the side, it was Pilot-Rescue No. 15 for them.

They keep box-score on it, just as carriers keep score of the planes they shoot down. They even keep records of their speed, and try to set a new record. They fished out Jimmy seven minutes after he went over. Their record rescue is three minutes.

On the destroyer they put Jimmy to bed, got the water out of him and some morphine into him, and sewed up the gash in his head. The doctor joked as he sewed, telling Jimmy he was sorry he couldn't find a bigger needle so it would hurt more.

Jimmy was nightmarish all night. He didn't get sick at his stomach until next morning, when he tried to get some breakfast down. He had a headache next day, but after that he was all right.

**PYLE**

Destroyers treat rescued pilots as though they were kings. They put Jimmy up in the skipper's private cabin, since the skipper was on the bridge day and night anyhow.

Jimmy wore the skipper's bathrobe and house slippers and underwear. The skipper came in a couple of times to take a bath, and actually apologized for intruding.

Fishing out pilots is such a frequent occurence that the skipper even keeps a bundle of brand new toothbrushes in his medicine cabinet for such sudden guests.

By the time Jimmy came to, the laundry had washed and pressed his clothes. He didn't have his wallet with him, so his pictures and private papers were spared a dunking.

This certain destroyer has fished out so many pilots that they have a scroll already printed up for such cases, and all they have to do is fill in the name. It's a picturesque certificate like you get when you cross the Equator.

Across the top of Jimmy's scroll was engraved the words—"The Blank's Home for Dripping Aviators."

And beneath it was this—"Know ye that Lt. James Van Fleet on such and such a date abruptly appeared, into our happy home, and due to the peculiarities of his arrival has been found worthy of being honored as a Blank's dripping aviator."

Engraved over the scroll was a huge arm reaching out from a destroyer, hauling a wet flier out of the ocean by the seat of his pants.

* * *

They returned Jimmy to us three days later, when they were delivering messages and mail from the flagship. They sent him over in a bosn's chair, pulled across on a heavy line strung between the two ships.

We got Jimmy aboard, and then we sent something back across in the bosn's chair to the destroyer. You'd never guess what it was. It was 20 gallons of ice cream!

Our carrier always does that when a destroyer rescues one of our pilots. Apparently all carriers don't, for the destroyer sent back a scribbled note saying "Thanks a lot. That is the nicest thing that has ever happened to us."

* * *

After Jimmy told me the whole story, we sent a signal back to the destroyer asking for the names of the two men who rescued him. The destroyer came right back:—

The swimmer was Seaman First Class Franklin Calloway, of 4633 Oakland St., Philadelphia, and the one who helped was Radioman Third Class Melvin Collins, of 102 North Vine St., Otumwa, Iowa.

They're smart on that destroyer. Because a few hours later there came another message saying, "If that information is for the press, might add that both men received Bronze Stars for similar rescue work during operations off Leyte last fall!"

* * *

Jimmy Van Fleet is 25, and incongruous as it seems, was a school teacher before he became a fighter pilot in the Navy. His home in Findlay is at 327 College St., but his wife is living at 339 N. Main St., Kenton (cq) Ohio. He has a son seven months old whom he has never seen.

Jimmy asked me if I had ever been in Vienna. He said that was his dad's "dream city." His father was a Pfc. in the last war, and spent three years in a hospital in Vienna, and has always wanted to go back.

These columns are probably the first news Jimmy's folks have had of his little mid-ocean escapade. It is glorious news alongside the last grave message they had.

For Jimmy's only brother, Ensign Donald Van Fleet, also a carrier pilot, was killed off Formosa just a few months ago. He had got two Jap planes in the two weeks before he himself was shot down. We are grateful that the sea gave Jimmy back.

PASSAIC, N. J., SATURDAY, OCTOBER 13, 1945

# BERGEN

## Garfield Sailor Tours Ruined Tokyo, Yokohama

### Through Letter, He Offers to Guide Home-Town Friends—Japan Desolate Place

**By Michael Supko**

WITH A GARFIELD NAVY MAN as a guide, we're going to take his friends and any Garfield resident who wishes, on a trip through Yokohama and Tokyo. Our guide is Michael Bak Jr., QM 1/c, who is serving on the USS Franks. His home is at 133 Semel Avenue. "My Liberty in Tokyo and Yokohama", is what he calls his letter.

Michael Supko

"Yesterday eighteen enlisted men and an officer of the Franks were granted liberty for the first time on the Japanese homeland, fifteen days after the Army landed. I was fortunate to be included in the first group and being the senior enlisted rated man, was designated as "Shore Patrol".

* * * * *

"American money had to be exchanged for Japanese currency by our supply officer who obtained the money from the customs house in Yokohama. One American dollar was exchanged for fifteen Yen in Jap money so the whole group went over with a fist full of Jap bills, cigarettes, candy bars, chewing gum and soap to trade with the Japs mainly for souvenirs.

"As the liberty party started walking down the dock there were many Japs in uniform trying to buy or trade for American cigarettes. To me it seems that the Japanese people start smoking when they are two years old. Everybody and his grandmother wanted our cigarettes. Every male, regardless of age, is in a uniform of some sort. They seem very small, dirty, greasy and sneaky, just as I always pictured them.

* * * * *

"As the party went along, ruins were visible on all sides for miles and miles with only a few scattered buildings and factories left undamaged. There was practically nothing left in Yokohama that is worthwhile to speak about. Some Japs were trying to sell some small trinkets as souvenirs, but the prices they asked were too high.

"Seven of us went ahead and started hitch hiking to Tokyo, twelve miles away. Transportation was practically at a standstill in Yokohama except for a few trolleys, cars and one or two trains which were always packed like sardine cans. The majority of civilians use bicycles, mules, horses and carts to get around. There were many of our Army trucks on the road to Tokyo so it was easy to get a ride.

* * * * *

"Traffic passes on the left side of the road. Only a few Jap cars were around, mostly operated by the Imperial Government. One Jap car passes us with several gold braided Jap officers who salute us as they went by. If I had my way, I would have told them something, but I returned the salute.

"The roads to Tokyo were awful with nothing along the way but ruins and more ruins. Many cars and trolleys were in ruins and most of the homes and factories level with the ground.

"Most civilians now live in dirty tin huts along the road, made from scraps gathered in the ruins. I can't for the life of me see where they get their food. Poverty is written all over them. Most of the Japs children would wave when they saw an American truck. They seemed glad to see us, but you could still notice a few who resented our being there. Why they ever continued to fight as long as they did is beyond me. They lost everything they had and it will take years to rebuild the ruins.

* * * * *

"Our B-29's did a complete job in Tokyo and Japs are still digging in the ruins.

"Every time one of our gang threw away a cigarette butt, there would be a scramble for it. There's nothing you can purchase for money in Tokyo, but you can get practically anything they have for cigarettes, candy, gum or soap. They paid 20 Yen for a pack of cigarettes. I sold a couple of packs to get the money as souvenirs. The Japs have loads of money in their wallets. Their clothing consists of burlap bags, rags, slacks, wooden shoes, with only a few dressed in American style.

"To have something to eat or drink, the sightseer must take along his own chow and water, otherwise go hungry. My chow was a canteen of water and two cheese sandwiches. Few understood our language. We had a grand time saying anything we wanted without them understanding. In return they would show a mouth full of teeth in a silly grin. Most of them step out of our way.

"The Japs must have mistaken me for an Admiral or something and kept pointing to my three stripes and SP band.

"As a whole, the Americans are treating them much better than they deserve."

Ships Data Section
Office of Public Information
Navy Department

## HISTORY OF USS FRANKS (DD 554)

On the first anniversary of Japan's sneak attack on Pearl Harbor, 7 December 1942, the 2000-ton flush-deck destroyer FRANKS slid down greased ways at the Seattle-Tacoma Shipbuilding Corporation's Puget Sound yards. Sponsoring the ship at the launching ceremonies was Mrs. Martha Carr, cousin of William J. Franks for whom the ship was named. W. J. Franks was a seaman aboard USS MARMORA at the attack on Yazoo City, Mississippi during the Civil War. He was awarded a Medal of Honor and promoted to Acting Master's Mate for gallantry in action while ashore on 5 March 1864 manning a howitzer against Confederate forces.

At the end of a six-month period the ship was ready for acceptance by the Navy and on 30 July 1943 she was commissioned USS FRANKS (DD 554), with Lieutenant Commander N. A. Lidstone, USN, as first commanding officer. Upon completion of final fitting-out she made ready for sea on 21 August and six days later she moved down coast to an operating area off San Diego where she, in company with cruiser OAKLAND and destroyer HOEL, conducted shakedown maneuvers commencing 30 August. On 9 September the ships unlimbered their main batteries for practice shore bombardment off San Clemente Island. Upon securing from these drills FRANKS returned to her home port in Puget Sound and on 30 September reported in for post shakedown yard availibility.

Upon completion of the yard period (15 October) the ship stood out for San Pedro from where she departed as a unit of Task Group 12.1 to arrive at Pearl Harbor on 26 October. While at Pearl the ship engaged in a series of drills, maneuvers and gunnery exercises as part of the staging for the forthcoming operation in the Gilbert Islands. This campaign was to initiate the offensive stage of the Pacific War and the amphibious operation was under the command of Lieutenant General Holland M. "Howlin' Mad" Smith, USMC.

After the pre-invasion shelling by the capital ships, the Marine landing force moved ashore on 20 November under the protection of escort-carrier launched naviators. During these landing operations FRANKS screened the flat-top operations as air-sea guard and anti-sub patrol. The only U. S. loss was escort-carrier LISCOME BAY which was torpedoed by a submarine on 24 November 1943.

FRANKS was then assigned to Task Force 53 on 1 December and spent the ensuing thirteen days patrolling the entrance to Tarawa Lagoon off Betio Island. In early January 1944 she retired to Pearl Harbor for minor voyage repairs.

On 22 January FRANKS and task force cleared Pearl for the Marshall Islands campaign and on 31 January the group was organized as anti-submarine patrol off Kwajalein. The landings went off on schedule and the island was secured on 5 February. FRANKS then engaged in close-in reconnaissance and bombardment of Ebeye Island where she was once under fire from gun emplacements ashore. At the end of this operation she returned to Pearl for another yard period.

On 4 March FRANKS stood out as escort unit for transport CLAY and arrived at Funafuti, Ellice Islands on 11 March. Upon being assigned to the Third Fleet, she proceeded to the Solomons and there operated out of Purvis Bay, Florida Island. On 23 March she moved close ashore at Mussau Island (north of New Ireland) where she bombarded an enemy gasoline dump; moving then to Kapingamaringi Atoll, the ship conducted close-in reconnaissance before returning to Purvis Bay.

The ensuing weeks were spent in convoy and patrol work in and around the Solomons and on 10 May the ship departed Treasury Island in company with Task Unit 30.6.2. While patrolling as screen for the mine layers working in Buka Passage, FRANKS got action on the night of 16-17 May when a submarine contact was made, destroyers JOHNSTON, HAGGARD and FRANKS receiving class "B" assessments for their attack. On 18 May the ship joined with the 35th Amphibious Group, Fifth Fleet and two days later steamed into the Solomon Sea and participated in the bombardment of Shortland Island. During this operation the ship was subjected to fire from enemy shore batteries. Retiring from this area, the ship moved then to the area of operation in the Marianas Islands. Here the latter part of June was spent patrolling off Guam with Task Group 53.2.

On 30 June 1944 Lieutenant Commander D. R. Stephen, USN, reported aboard and relieved Commander Lidstone as skipper of FRANKS.

With the new commanding officer aboard, FRANKS retired from the forward area and arrived 3 July at Eniwetok for supplies and logistics, returning to the Marianas to participate in bombardment and night harassing fire on Guam beginning 12 July. On the night of the 14th the ship was the target for a bombing and strafing run by an enemy plane;

however, the bomb hit some 200 yards astern and no damage was sustained. On 9 August FRANKS departed for Eniwetok and retired then to Espiritu Santo, arriving 24 August.

In mid-September she participated in the Palau Islands operations, moving then to aid in the acquisition of Ulithi Atoll on 24 September. At Seeadler Harbor, Manus, Admiralty Islands, FRANKS joined Task Group 77.4 on 8 October and operated with this group during initial strikes on the Philippines. The destroyer was present during the Battle of Leyte Gulf on 24-25 October as a member of Admiral T. C. Kinkaid's force. While operating in the Philippine area she rescued survivors of three downed planes.

On 23 November 1944 FRANKS was detached from Task Unit 77.4.6 and early in December was assigned to Task Force 38 in which she operated with the carriers supporting the Mindoro occupation; during January 1945 she operated with Task Units 38.2.3 and 38.2.10 (Night Carrier Group), supporting landings on Luzon by air strikes on Formosa and in the South China Sea.

On 27 January FRANKS was assigned to Task Group 58.4 and after undergoing routine availibility at Ulithi until 9 February, departed for the area off Honshu where the task force launched strikes against the Japanese Empire in support of the assault and occupation of Iwo Jima, Bonin Islands, to the south. During this period of operation the ship picked up two more pilots. At the end of February the force retired to Ulithi where FRANKS remained until 14 March.

Getting underway again on this date, Task Force 58 departed for strikes against Kyushu and Nansei Shoto in support of the assault and occupation of Okinawa Gunt. At 0730 on 18 March enemy air attacks commenced and continued throughout the day and FRANKS was credited with shooting down one plane and registering three "assists." On the 24th she screened battleships during the bombardment of the south coast of Okinawa, which was a diversionary move to cover the beaches selected for U. S. landings, the western beaches. Three days later she operated with a group in a night shelling sorties at Daito Shima.

In late afternoon of 2 April, while steaming about 100 miles off the east coast of Okinawa, FRANKS secured from her air-sea rescue station as the last of the planes were landed. In maneuvering for her assigned running screen position, she collided with battleship NEW JERSEY (incidentally, launched the same day as FRANKS). The initial impact demolished all port side armament and the bridge wing. Commander D. R. Stephen, commanding officer, was fatally injured and Lieutenant G. F. Case, USN, the executive officer assumed command.

The following morning FRANKS retired to Ulithi where temporary repairs were effected. On 13 April, in company with baby-carrier CABOT and bombscarred carrier HANCOCK, she got underway for Pearl Harbor, arriving on 21 April.

On 22 April 1945 Lieutenant Commander E. B. Henry, Jr., USN, reported aboard as new commanding officer and Lieutenant Case resumed duties as executive officer. The same day, FRANKS departed independently for Puget Sound Navy Yard for a complete overhaul, arriving Bremerton, Washington on 29 April.

Having completed overhaul and readiness for sea trials, FRANKS departed 30 June for an underway training period off San Diego. At the end of this training, she departed on 12 July in company with destroyer SWANSON and arrived at Pearl Harbor on 18 July. More training exercises followed at Pearl and on 10 August she stood out for Eniwetok with destroyers KIMBERLY, HALSEY POWELL and YARNALL. While underway on 15 August, news of Japan's capitulation arrived and two days later the ships reported for duty with the Third Fleet at Eniwetok.

On 19 August destroyers FRANKS and DUNCAN departed Eniwetok screening escort-carriers ATTU and SITKOH BAY and proceeded to an operating area southeast of Honshu where, on 3 September, the ships rendezvoused with Task Force 38. FRANKS was ordered to an air-sea rescue station southwest of Honshu where hourly weather reports were sent out for plane traffic between Okinawa and Tokyo. She steamed on this station until 10 September when she was relieved and assigned to Task Group 38.1. She joined this unit off the east coast of Honshu on the 11th and five days later entered Tokyo Bay for a period of availibility.

On 1 October 1945 FRANKS stood out of Tokyo Bay, with whistle blowing, enroute for the West Coast, via Okinawa. She arrived at Seattle, Washington on 19 October and after a brief brass-polishing period, moved to Astoria, Washington to participate in the Navy Day celebration. On 1 November 1945 she steamed down coast to San Pedro and was there submitted to a yard availibility period.

USS FRANKS (DD 554) was placed out of commission in reserve on 31 May 1946, and at present (16 January 1948) is a member of the San Diego Reserve Group.

\* \* \*

USS FRANKS earned nine battle stars for participation in the following operations and engagements:

1 star/Gilbert Islands Operations -- 20 Nov. to 8 Dec. 1943

1 star/Marshall Islands Operation -- 1944
    Occupation of Kwajalein and Majuro Atolls -- 5-8 Feb. 1943

1 star/"B" Assessment in submarine action on 16 May 1944

1 star/Marianas Operation -- 1944
    Capture and Occupation of Saipan - 16-18 July 1944
    Capture and Occupation of Guam - 12 July to 9 Aug. 1944

1 star/Western Caroline Islands Operation --
    Capture and Occupation of the Southern Palau Islands --
    6 September to 14 October 1944

1 star/Leyte Operation - 1944
    Leyte Landings -- 10 October to 29 November 1944
    Luzon Attacks -- 14-16 December 1944

1 star/Luzon Operation - 1944-45
    Luzon Attacks - 6-7 January 1945
    Fifth Fleet Raids against Honshu and the Nansei
      Shoto -- 15-16, 25 February and 1 March 1945

1 star/Okinawa Gunto Operation -- 1945
    Fifth and Third Fleet Raids in support of Okinawa
      Gunto Operation -- 17 March to 2 April 1945

\* \* \*

## STATISTICS

| | | |
|---|---|---|
| LENGTH | 376 feet | ARMAMENT - Five 5-inch/38 calibre dual purpose mounts. 40- and 20-mm AA batteries. 10 21-inch torpedo tubes. |
| EXTREME BEAM | 39 feet | |
| DISPLACEMENT | 2050 tons | |
| CREW | 300 plus | |
| SPEED | 35 knots-plus | |

Stencilled 16 Jan. 1948

Index

to

Reminiscences of

Mr. Michael Bak, Jr.

Air Forces, U.S. Army
    Reluctant to take non-college men as pilots early in World War II, p. 18; B-29 strikes against Japan in early 1945 impressed Navymen in ships below, p. 191

Antiair Warfare
    The destroyer Franks (DD-554) frequently fired at Japanese planes during World War II, pp. 123-127, 183-185; a Japanese plane just missed bombing the Franks near Guam in July 1944, p. 151

Antisubmarine Warfare (ASW)
    Practiced during shakedown training of the crew of the destroyer Franks (DD-554) in 1943, p. 55; the Franks helped sink a Japanese submarine in May 1944, pp. 129, 139-140

Army, U.S.
    Bak enjoyed visiting his cousin Daniel Serafin, an Army enlisted man, in Hawaii in 1943, pp. 78-87; soldiers in Japan in late 1945 sold goods on the black market, pp. 224-225

Astoria, Oregon
    The destroyer Franks (DD-554) and cruiser Pittsburgh (CA-72) visited this city for Navy Day 1945, pp. 230-231

Athletics
    Bak's participation in New Jersey in the 1930s and 1940s, pp. 5-6, 9

Atomic Bombs
    Reaction on board the destroyer Franks (DD-554) to the dropping of bombs on Japan in August 1945, pp. 219-220

Aviators
    Rescued by the destroyer Franks (DD-554) in World War II, pp. 74-76, 93-94, 120-121, 133-134, 177-181

B-29s
    Bombing runs toward Japan in early 1945 impressed Navy men in the ships below, p. 191

Bak, Michael, Jr.
    Boyhood in New Jersey in 1920s and 1930s, pp. 1-14; son of Russian immigrants with little knowledge of English, pp. 1-7, 11-14, 20-21, 62; education of in New Jersey in the 1930s and 1940s, pp. 6, 11, 13; participated in athletics in New Jersey in the 1930s and 1940s, pp. 5-6, 9; employment in civilian jobs in 1941-42 in New Jersey, pp. 15-16; enlistment in the Navy in December 1942, pp. 17-21; recruit training at Great Lakes in early 1943, pp. 21-32; training in quartermaster rating at Great Lakes in early

1943, pp. 32-37; experiences around Bremerton, Washington, after reporting to the destroyer Franks (DD-554) in July 1943, pp. 37-49; exchange of mail with family, pp. 61-63; had enjoyable visit to Hawaii in 1943 while on the way to the war zone, pp. 78-89; experienced first combat during the Gilbert Islands invasion in November 1943, pp. 91-96; typical day as quartermaster in the war zone, pp. 94-98, 103-105; initiation on crossing equator, pp. 101-103; steering of the Franks during refueling at sea, pp. 109-111; got rid of a former girlfriend through a letter to his family, pp. 117-118; reaction to being under air attack while on board the Franks, pp. 123-127; missed 21st birthday in 1944 because of crossing the international date line, p. 129; concerned about personal safety during the Battle of Leyte Gulf in October 1944, pp. 156-158; attitude about the war during a break from combat in late 1944-early 1945, pp. 169-170; attended religious services when opportunities permitted, pp. 174-176; made an enjoyable trip home to New Jersey on leave in the spring of 1945, pp. 206-213; ashore on liberty in Japan in late 1945, pp. 223-230; release from naval service in 1946 and summary of civilian career in the years since then, pp. 234-242

Barbee, Signalman Second Class John
Served on signal bridge of the destroyer Franks (DD-554) in World War II, pp. 106-107, 136-137

Boot camp
Former ballplayer Fred Lindstrom was company commander at Great Lakes in early 1943, pp. 21-22; training for shipboard duty, pp. 22-23, 28-31; liberty in Milwaukee was enjoyable, pp. 23-25; recruits slept in hammocks in barracks, pp. 26-27

Bremerton, Washington
USS Franks (DD-554) was completed and put into commission at the Puget Sound Navy Yard in July 1943, pp. 37-38, 43; post-shakedown yard period for the Franks in 1943, pp. 70-71; repairs to the Franks in the summer of 1945, pp. 215-216

Case, Lieutenant Gerald F., USN
Officer who served as a department head and later as temporary commanding officer of the destroyer Franks (DD-554) in World War II, pp. 148, 201-202

Censorship
Officers censored enlisted men's mail on board the destroyer Franks (DD-554) in World War II, pp. 63, 105

Charts--Navigation
   Updating of charts on board the destroyer Franks (DD-554) in World War II, p. 71; not always reliable when the ship was in remote locations, p. 94

Collisions
   The destroyer Franks (DD-554) and battleship New Jersey (BB-62) collided off Okinawa on 2 April 1945, pp. 193-196

Crabbe, Lieutenant Commander C.R., USNR
   USS Franks (DD-554) executive officer who went overboard from the ship in 1945, pp. 199-200

Deck Logs
   Material included in ship's logs on board the destroyer Franks (DD-554) in World War II, pages 53-55

Equator-Crossing Initiation
   On board the destroyer Franks (DD-554) in late 1943, pp. 101-103

Food
   Good meals provided to recruits at Great Lakes boot camp in early 1943, pp. 27-28; men of the destroyer Franks (DD-554) complained of too much steak to eat in mid-1943, p. 40; quality of chow on board the Franks, pp. 119-120; eating posed challenges when the Franks was rolling, pp. 165-167; the crew of the Franks was rewarded with ice cream when the ship returned a downed aviator to his carrier, p. 179

Forer, Lieutenant (junior grade) David, USNR
   Competent officer who served as navigator of the destroyer Franks (DD-554) in World War II, pp. 72-75

Franks, USS (DD-554)
   Work on this destroyer was nearing completion when Bak reported for duty in July 1943, pp. 37-38; living conditions for the crew, pp. 38-40, 59-60, 116-117; crew liberty in the Bremerton-Seattle, Washington, area in July 1943, pp. 40-43; relationship between officers and enlisted crew members, pp. 45-46, 98, 105, 132-133, 149-151; Commander Nicholas Lidstone was a quiet, competent commanding officer in 1943-44, pp. 46-47, 77-78, 112-113, 145; commissioning on 30 July 1943, p. 48; crew members felt privileged to serve in a Fletcher (DD-445)-class destroyer, pp. 48-49; shakedown training off the West Coast in the summer of 1943, pp. 49-57; attitudes of crew members in 1943 when going to war for the first time, pp. 57-58, 61; main form of recreation was chatting with fellow crew members, pp. 60-61, 106; importance of mail to the crew, pp. 61-63; quartermaster gang put in long hours on the bridge, pp. 65-66; the ship was darkened topside at night during wartime, pp. 67-68; post-shakedown yard period at Bremerton in 1943, pp. 70-71; celestial navigation, p. 73-

74; rescue of downed aviators in World War II, pp. 74-76; 120-121, 133-134; stopped in Hawaii in 1943 while on the way to the war zone, pp. 78-89; crew's attitude toward the Japanese after stop in Pearl Harbor, pp. 87-88; support of the Gilbert Islands invasion in November 1943 included being nearby when the escort carrier Liscome Bay (CVE-56) was torpedoed and sunk, pp. 91-96; typical day for a quartermaster in the war zone, pp. 94-98, 103-105; attitude of crew members in 1944, after having been in battle, p. 101; crossing-the-equator ceremony in late 1943, pp. 101-103; crew members had few opportunities to spend their pay while at sea, pp. 107-109; steering of the ship during refueling at sea, pp. 109-111; quality of food on board, pp. 119-120; the ship returned to Pearl Harbor for upkeep and liberty in late 1943, following the Gilberts campaign, pp. 121-122; the Franks frequently fired at Japanese aircraft during World War II, pp. 123-127; handling characteristics in rough seas, pp. 128; discipline of the crew during World War II, pp. 131-132; enlisted men on board were not particularly conscious of petty officer rates, pp. 135-136; bombarded the island of Mussau in March 1944, pp. 138-139; helped sink a Japanese submarine in the Solomons in May 1944, pp. 139-140; involvement in the Marianas campaign in the spring of 1944, pp. 143-144; information about war progress given to crew, pp. 144-145; Commander David R. Stephen was a demanding, energetic skipper during his command tenure from June 1944 to April 1945, pp. 146-150, 158, 160, 171-172; crew had liberty in Ulithi Atoll in 1944-45, pp. 152-154; the Franks was one of a number of U.S. warships attacked by Japanese surface forces at Leyte Gulf in late October 1944, pp. 127, 154-161; rolled heavily during the big typhoon off the Philippines in December 1944, pp. 161-166; destroyermen developed methods for eating when the ship was rolling, pp. 165-167; storm damage repaired at Ulithi in early 1945, pp. 168-169, 173; operations with aircraft carriers in early 1945, pp. 176-186, 190-191; crew attitude about chances for survival, pp. 184-185; involved in the Iwo Jima operation in February 1945, pp. 187-189; involved in the Okinawa operation in March-April 1945, pp. 192-193; collision with the USS New Jersey (BB-62) pp. 193-196; death and burial of the commanding officer in April 1945, pp. 196-199; executive officer C.R. Crabbe lost overboard, pp. 199-200; Lieutenant Gerald Case succeeded to command after Stephen's death, pp. 201-202; collision repairs at Ulithi, pp. 202-204; trip back to the United States and repairs at Bremerton, pp. 204-207, 215-216; crew turnover, p. 216; events surrounding the end of the war in the Pacific, pp. 218-223; occupation duty in Japan provided opportunity for crew liberty, pp. 223-230; return to the United States and demobilization of crew, pp. 230-235

Gambling
    Done by the crew of the destroyer Franks (DD-554) during

World War II, pp. 42, 58-59

Gilbert Islands
   Destroyer Franks (DD-554) was part of the invasion support force in November 1943 and nearby when the Liscome Bay (CVE-56) was sunk, pp. 91-96

Grace, Chief Quartermaster Justin, USN
   Provided training to new men on board the destroyer Franks (DD-554) in 1943, pp. 43-44, 114-115; apparently resented junior quartermasters who made rate much faster than he had, pp. 98-100; involved in equator initiation in late 1943, p. 103; steering of the ship during refueling at sea, pp. 109-110; resentful toward the commanding officer, p. 112

Great Lakes, Illinois
   Location of recruit training for Bak in early 1943, pp. 21-32; location of quartermaster training for Bak in early 1943, pp. 32-37

Gunnery--Naval
   The USS Franks (DD-554) trained her gun crews during shakedown off the West Coast in the summer of 1943, pp. 52, 55-56; various antiaircraft actions in which the ship was involved during World War II, pp. 123-127, 183; shore bombardment by the Franks, pp. 141-142, 188-189, 192

Habitability
   Recruits slept in hammocks at boot camp in Great Lakes, Illinois, in early 1943, pp. 26-27; crowded compartments and small lockers on board the destroyer Franks (DD-554), to which Bak reported in July 1943, pp. 38-39, 59-60, 116-117; conditions at the Army's Schofield barracks in Hawaii in 1943, pp. 86-87

Halsey, Admiral William F., Jr., USN (USNA, 1904)
   As Commander Third Fleet in 1944-45, he instilled confidence in those serving under him, p. 186; and the Japanese surrender in 1945, p. 221

Hawaii
   Bak had enjoyable experiences on liberty with cousin Daniel Serafin on Oahu in 1943, pp. 78-89; the Franks (DD-554) made a brief visit to Pearl in late 1943, pp. 121-122

Henry, Lieutenant Commander Eugene B., USN (USNA, 1939)
   Became commanding officer of the destroyer Franks (DD-554) in 1945 after previous skipper was killed, pp. 206-207, 217

Honolulu, Hawaii
   Bak had enjoyable experiences here on liberty with cousin Daniel Serafin in 1943, pp. 78-89

I-176
    Japanese submarine sunk by U.S. destroyers in the Solomons in May 1944, pp. 139-140

Iwo Jima
    The destroyer Franks (DD-554) supported the 1945 invasion of this island with shore bombardment, pp. 187-189

Japan
    Occupation of by U.S. forces in 1945, pp. 221-223; sailors from destroyer Franks (DD-554) ashore in Japan on liberty in 1945, pp. 223-230

Johnston, USS (DD-557)
    Destroyer sunk 25 October 1944 in the Battle of Leyte Gulf, pp. 144, 155, 157, 159

Kalakala
    Ferryboat which took sailors from Bremerton to Seattle, Washington, for liberty in mid-1943, p. 42

Leave and Liberty
    Bak found Milwaukee to be an extremely hospitable city for servicemen on liberty in early 1943, pp. 23-25; crewmen of the destroyer Franks (DD-554) went on liberty in the Bremerton-Seattle, Washington, area in mid-1943, pp. 40-43; sight-seeing was the primary attraction in Southern California in the summer of 1943, pp. 63-65; Bak had an enjoyable reunion with cousin Daniel Serafin while on liberty in Hawaii in 1943, pp. 78-89; the forward area offered a few opportunities for liberty in such places as Ulithi and New Guinea in 1944-45, pp. 152-154; Bak made an enjoyable trip home to New Jersey on leave in the spring of 1945, pp. 206-213; liberty in Seattle, Washington, in the summer of 1945, pp. 214-215; men from the Franks ashore in Japan in late 1945, pp. 223-230; in Astoria, Oregon, in late October 1945, pp. 230-231; in the Los Angeles area in late 1945-early 1946, pp. 232-234

Lewis, Signalman Charles
    Sailor from the destroyer Franks (DD-554) who was accepted for flight training in World War II, pp. 64, 232, 234

Leyte Gulf, Battle of
    The destroyer Franks (DD-554) was one of the ships which came under attack by Japanese surface forces, pp. 127, 154-161

Liberty
    See Leave and Liberty

Lidstone, Commander Nicholas A., USN (USNA, 1930)
   Quiet, competent professional who commanded the destroyer *Franks* (DD-554) in 1943-44, pp. 46-47, 77-78, 107, 112-113, 145; involved in rescue of downed aviators, p. 76

Lindstrom, Frederick C.
   Former major league ballplayer who served as a boot camp company commander at Great Lakes, Illinois, in 1943, pp. 21-22

*Liscome Bay*, USS (CVE-56)
   Escort carrier sunk on 23 November 1943 during the Gilbert Islands operation, pp. 61, 91-93, 96

Logs
   Material included in ship's deck logs on board the destroyer *Franks* (DD-554) in World War II, pp. 53-55

Mail
   Very important for morale of sailors on board the destroyer *Franks* (DD-554) in World War II, pp. 61-63; censorship by *Franks* officers, pp. 63, 105; Bak got rid of a former girlfriend through a letter to his family from the *Franks*, pp. 117-118

Marianas Campaign
   Involvement by the destroyer *Franks* (DD-554) in the spring of 1944, pp. 143-144; a Japanese plane just missed bombing the *Franks* near Guam in July 1944, p. 151

Medical Problems
   Sailors warned at Great Lakes boot camp in 1943 about the danges of venereal disease, p. 41

Milwaukee, Wisconsin
   City that was extremely hospitable to visiting servicemen in World War II, pp. 23-25

Mussau
   Pacific Island bombarded by the destroyer *Franks* (DD-554) in March 1944, pp. 138-139

Navigation
   Training in various aspects of navigation included in quartermaster school at Great Lakes in early 1943, pp. 32-37; piloting of the destroyer *Franks* (DD-554) in coastal waters in 1943, pp. 49-50; updating of charts, p. 71; celestial navigation on board the *Franks* during World War II, pp. 73-74, 104-105; importance of position accuracy in shore bombardment, pp. 188-189

New Guinea
   The crew of the destroyer *Franks* (DD-554) had liberty briefly at Hollandia in 1944, p. 154

New Jersey, USS (BB-62)
   Collided with the destroyer Franks (DD-554) off Okinawa on 2 April 1945, pp. 59, 193-196; flagship for Admiral William Halsey, p. 186

Norman Scott, USS (DD-690)
   Destroyer which recovered officer who had gone overboard from the USS Franks (DD-554) in early 1945, pp. 199-200

Okinawa
   Support of invasion by the destroyer Franks (DD-554) in March-April 1945, pp. 192-196

O'Neill, Ensign John H., USNR
   USS Franks (DD-554) officer who took a pistol from a recovered U.S. aviator in World War II, pp. 177-178

Pay and Allowances
   Crew of the destroyer Franks (DD-554) didn't have many opportunities for spending money while at sea in World War II, pp. 107-109

Pearl Harbor, Hawaii
   Bak had an enjoyable visit with cousin Daniel Serafin while on liberty in Hawaii in 1943, pp. 78-89; the Franks (DD-554) had a brief stop at Pearl in late 1943, pp. 121-122

Piedmont, USS (AD-17)
   Destroyer tender which repaired typhoon-damaged ships at Ulithi in early 1945, pp. 168-169, 173

Pilots
   Rescued by the destroyer Franks (DD-554) in World War II, pp. 74-76, 93-94, 120-121, 133-134, 177-181

Plane Guard Duty
   The destroyer Franks (DD-554) rescued more than 20 downed pilots while operating with aircraft carriers in World War II, pp. 74-76, 93-94, 120-121, 133-134, 177-181

Prostitution
   Long lines of servicemen waited in line for their turn to be with prostitutes in Honolulu in 1943, pp. 82-83

Puget Sound Navy Yard, Bremerton, Washington
   USS Franks (DD-554) was completed and put into commission at this shipyard in July 1943, pp. 37-38, 43; post-shakedown yard period for the Franks in 1943, pp. 70-71; repairs to the Franks in the summer of 1945, pp. 215-216

Pyle, Ernie
   U.S. war correspondent who wrote of naval operations in early 1945, pp. 181-182

Quartermaster Rating
   Bak received training in various aspects of the rating in school at Great Lakes, Illinois, in early 1943, pp. 32-37; Chief Justin Grace provided training to new men on board the destroyer Franks (DD-554) in 1943, pp. 43-44; quartermasters in the Franks learned a lot by virtue of their duty station on the bridge, pp. 47-48; duties involved in maintaining the ship's deck log, pp. 53-54; long hours on the bridge cut into sleep time, pp. 65-66; typical day for a quartermaster on board the Franks in World War II, pp. 94-98, 103-105; relationship between the quartermasters and boatswain's mates on board the Franks, pp. 115-116; responsible for operating battle lights from the bridge, p. 130; quartermasters of the Franks not particularly rank-conscious, p. 136

Recruit Training
   Former ballplayer Fred Lindstrom was a company commander at Great Lakes in early 1943, pp. 21-22; training for shipboard duty, pp. 22-23, 28-31; liberty in Milwaukee was enjoyable, pp. 23-25; recruits slept in hammocks in barracks, pp. 26-27

Refueling at Sea
   Factors involved in steering the destroyer Franks (DD-554) during World War II refueling operations, pp. 109-111; hazardous operation during 1944 typhoon, p. 162, 164

Religion
   Bak was brought up in the Russian Orthodox Church in New Jersey in the 1930s, p. 5; men from small ships attended services on board large ships in World War II, pp. 174-176

Sand Point Naval Air Station, Seattle, Washington
   Planes from this air station were involved in the training of the new destroyer Franks (DD-554) in the summer of 1943, p. 51

Serafin, Corporal Daniel, USA
   Army enlisted man with whom Bak had enjoyable liberties in Hawaii in 1943, pp. 78-87

Ship's Logs
   Material included in deck logs on board the destroyer Franks (DD-554) in World War II, pp. 53-55

Shore Patrol
   Very much in evidence in Honolulu in 1943, pp. 81-83

Signaling--Visual
   Signalmen on board the destroyer Franks (DD-554) used infrared lamps for night signaling in World War II, p. 68; quartermaster Bak involved in signaling on board the Franks, pp. 106-107, 137; means for friends to communicate informally while their ships were at anchor, pp. 152-153

Snell, Ensign W.A., USNR
   USS Franks (DD-554) officer who retrieved debris after the sinking of the Japanese submarine I-176 in May 1944, p. 140

Stephan, Commander David R., USN (USNA, 1933)
   As commanding officer of the destroyer Franks (DD-554) in World War II, refused to allow Bak to leave the ship for flight training, p. 64; changed technique on rescue of downed aviators, p. 76; changed helmsmen for refueling operations because of parted hoses, pp. 109-110; informed crew of the Franks concerning war actions, p. 144, 171-172; demanding and aggressive as skipper of the Franks, pp. 146-150, 158, 160, 200-201; kept the Franks afloat during the great typhoon of December 1944, pp. 164-165; death and burial of following a collision with the battleship New Jersey (BB-62) in April 1945, pp. 196-199

Submarines
   The Japanese I-175 sank the escort carrier Liscome Bay (CVE-56) in November 1943, during the Gilbert Islands campaign, pp. 61, 91-93, 96; the Japanese I-176 was sunk by U.S. destroyers in the Solomons in May 1944, pp. 139-140

Tarawa
   The destroyer Franks (DD-554) was part of the invasion support force in November 1943, pp. 91-96

Third Naval District
   Bak's enlistment at district headquarters in New York City in December 1942, pp. 17-21

Thorson, Ensign R.J., USNR
   Criticized fellow officers on board the destroyer Franks (DD-554) during 1944, pp. 132-133

Tokyo Rose
   Radio broadcaster whose comments during World War II amused the crew of the destroyer Franks (DD-554), p. 187

Training
   Boot camp provided recruit training at Great Lakes, Illinois, in early 1943, pp. 21-32; quartermaster school at Great Lakes in early 1943 covered various duties of the rating, pp. 32-37; Chief Quartermaster Justin Grace provided training to new men of the destroyer Franks (DD-554) in 1943, pp. 43-44, 114-115; shakedown cruise for the crew of the new Franks in the summer of 1943, pp. 49-57; final preparation of the Franks crew for combat in the autumn of 1943, pp. 88-90, 95-96

Typhoons
   The destroyer Franks (DD-554) rolled heavily and had difficulty steering while in the typhoon off the Philippines in December 1944, pp. 161-166; damage to the Franks and Haggard (DD-555) repaired at Ulithi, pp. 168-169

Ulithi Atoll
   Fleet anchorage which also served as a recreation and repair area for U.S. warships and their crews in 1944-45, pp. 152-154; served as site for repair of typhoon damage to the USS Franks (DD-554) in early 1945, pp. 168-169, 173; repairs to the Franks in April 1945 after her collision with the USS New Jersey (BB-62), pp. 202-204

Uniforms--Naval
   Uniforms issued to recruits at boot camp in early 1943, p. 27; the crew of the destroyer Franks (DD-554) wore dungarees in battle during World War II, pp. 130-131

United Services Organization
   Provided welcome recreation for sailors on liberty in Milwaukee in early 1943, pp. 24-25

USO
   See United Services Organization

Venereal Disease
   Sailors warned about health hazards at Great Lakes boot camp in 1943, p. 41

Visual Signaling
   Signalmen on board the destroyer Franks (DD-554) used infrared lamps for night signaling in World War II, p. 68; quartermaster Bak involved in signaling on board the Franks, pp. 106-107, 137; means for friends to communicate informally while their ships were at anchor, pp. 152-153

Weather
   The destroyer Franks (DD-554) went through the great typhoon of December 1944 off the Philippines, pp. 161-166

Wild, Gunner's Mate Second Class Thomas A., Jr.
   Headed a 40-mm. gun crew on board the destroyer Franks (DD-554) during World War II, p. 126

Yorktown, USS (CV-10)
   Bombed by Japanese aircraft on 18 March 1945, pp. 123, 126; operation off Okinawa in April 1945, pp. 193, 195

## WRECK ON THE FOC'SCLE

Wreck on the foc'scle
it happened one night
Saw the New Jersey
Coming in sight.

She climbed on our little bow
Raked us fore and aft
Left us asitting like
a broken down raft.

No forties on the port side
No number 2 stack
We got our orders, Boys
And are heading back.

Towed by the big tug
Towed all the way
Some way to sail, Boys
Anchors Aweigh

Rolled all the night
and Rolled all the day
Won!t be long 'til
We're in the U.S.A.

    by - Lt.(jg) Jack O'Neill
        USS Franks - 554
          Pacific - WW 11

www.ingramcontent.com/pod-product-compliance
Lightning Source LLC
Chambersburg PA
CBHW080615170426
43209CB00007B/1439